Small Courtesies

The Connoisseur Collection of Evelyn Ackerman

Theriault's
the dollmasters

Introduction

A passion for antique dolls offers the collector a glimpse into 'other people's lives' from past times and other places. Yet turn those three words around. Now think 'people's other lives'. Who was the collector that assembled these dolls? What was her life, her other occupations, her talents, her dreams? And how did her 'other life' complement, compliment, or contradict her love of dolls?

For Evelyn Ackerman of Los Angeles a love of antique dolls seems, at first, a contradiction. After all, here was a woman considered to be a pioneer in the mid-century California modernism art movement, a woman whose own designs have been described as *"optimistic, gorgeous, influenced by a sense of freedom"* by no less than the renown designer Jonathan Adler, and *"modernism at its warmest and most creative"* in *Handcrafted Modern: At Home with Mid-Century Designers* (Rizzoli, 2010). A New York Times article of January 2011 lauded Evelyn for her *"unique vision"*. Indeed, so influential have been her textile, mosaic and wood designs that the works of Evelyn and her husband Jerry were featured in an important retrospective exhibition "Masters of Mid-Century California Modernism" at the Mingei International Museum in San Diego in 2009, and again in a retrospective at the Craft and Folk Art Museum of Los Angeles in 2011. The Ackermans hold the rare distinction of being included in every exhibition (1954 to 1976) of the prestigious "California Design" show.

Evelyn Ackerman, early years in Los Angeles.

Evelyn and Jerry Ackerman.

This extraordinary and celebrated 'other life' may come as a surprise to those who have been fortunate enough to know Evelyn in the world of dolls where she has been celebrated as a prescient and stalwart researcher, author and connoisseur collector. Her published works in this field have not only included studies on Schoenhut's Humpty Dumpty Circus, but also the important books, *Dolls in Miniature* (Gold Horse Publishing, 1991) and *The Genius of Moritz Gottschalk* (Gold Horse Publishing, 1994), as well as numerous articles in industry publications including Miniature Collector, The Inside Collector, Dolls, Doll News, Doll Reader, and Antique Doll Collector. Given her prodigious output in the world of dolls, it is no wonder that collectors might not imagine her rich and rewarding other life.

Yet it was her prescient artist's eye that gave Evelyn the vision to see the infinite within the finite when it came to her choices of antique dolls and playthings. A dollhouse, to Evelyn, for example, was not merely a home and its furnishings, but also the inhabitants who peopled that home. As John Darcy Noble, Curator Emeritus of The Toy Collection of the City of New York noted in his foreword to her *Dolls in Miniature* book, "*…never before has there been a book whose focus is not so much on the houses, as on the dolls that were made to live in them. On reflection, this seems extraordinary, for the dolls are surely the very breath of life in a dolls' house, just as it is the inhabitants themselves who make real-life houses so fascinating*". This was not accidental. Evelyn, herself, expressed this concept

Evelyn Ackerman's work ranged from wood, to mosaic, to tapestry.

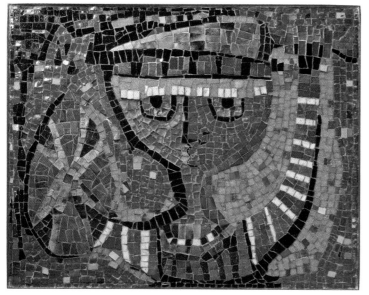

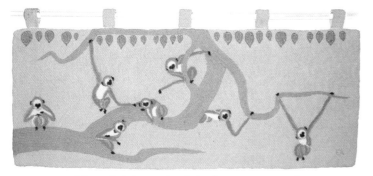

Ackerman's designs are described as, "gorgeous, optimistic."

in her own introduction to that book, noting that a dollhouse without dolls was just a quiet environment, but make one small change by adding a doll – just one doll – and *"suddenly life-bursting forces are evident"* and… *"imagination can restructure the perceived reality, giving it unlimited rein"*.

Throughout the years, dolls and toys and all the ephemera of childhoods past came to fill the home of Evelyn Ackerman. Her particular quest was deliberate. It was always for those objects that could give free rein to one's imagination. Why was this doll constructed in a certain way? Why was that doll, whose costume was so surely original, seemingly incongruous to its perceived place in society? Of what did the doll artist dream? A study of these dolls, in the mind and eye of Evelyn Ackerman, gave voice to the abstract, whimsical and quixotic, as well as the purely factual.

And thus, as surely as 18th century dolls and toys seem at first to be from a totally other world than mid-20th century modernist decorative art, a pattern begins to emerge that explains the artistic sensibility of Evelyn Ackerman. Although her own unique designs across a range of media, from woven and hooked wall hangings to tile mosaics to carved wood, have been eagerly sought by wealthy aesthetes, it was her belief that art should be made available – and affordable – to all. Inspired by the Bauhaus belief that fine and applied arts were equally important, she and Jerry uprooted from their native

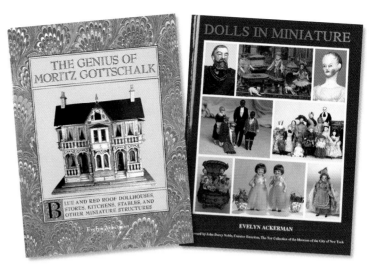

Detroit in 1952 and moved to Los Angeles where they opened Jenev Design Studios followed by Era Industries, at first creating singular art pieces and later commissioning the production of Evelyn's designs from skilled craftsmen in Greece, Kashmir, Italy, Japan and Mexico.

Dale Carolyn Gluckman, former associate curator Los Angeles County Museum of Art, wrote in her introduction to *The Genius of Moritz Gottschalk* that "*Mrs. Ackerman has drawn a picture of the ingenuity and creativity that went into an essentially commercial product*" and concludes "*This book shows us that even the smallest, most mundane objects of daily life can provide immense aesthetic satisfaction and shed light on their time*".

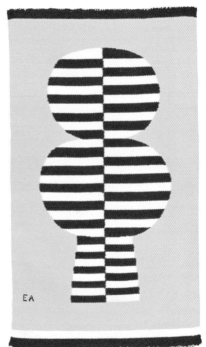

Top: covers of two books by Evelyn Ackerman, with her own cover designs.

Bringing art and beauty to all, combining the aesthetic with the affordable, meshing studio art with commercial production, influencing fine arts with folk arts, has been a central theme of the life of Evelyn Ackerman. It is apparent that her life as a collector and her 'other life' as a designer were intricately interwoven, never a contradiction, but always a complement and a compliment. We can all see more clearly through her vision. ❧

1. Rare Petite French Bisque Bébé, Figure C, by Jules Steiner with Au Nain Bleu Bonnet

8 ½" (22 cm.) Bisque socket head, blue glass paperweight inset eyes, painted lashes, feathered brows, accented nostrils, closed mouth with accent line between the full lips, waist-length mohair wig over original Steiner pate, Steiner composition fully-jointed body with straight wrists. Condition: generally excellent. Marks: Steiner Paris Fre C 4/0 (head) (Steiner stamp on body). Comments: Jules Steiner, circa 1880. Value Points: rare model in wonderful diminutive size, having lovely bisque and painting, original body and body finish, with original muslin

chemise and having woven bonnet with blue silk lining and blue band gilt lettered "Le Tapaceur" and with the label of the prestigious Parisian doll shop "Au Nain Bleu" on the interior. $2500/3500

2. Three English Poured Wax Miniature Dolls in Original Costumes

5" (13 cm.) Each has wax shoulder head, firmly-stuffed muslin body and wax lower limbs, including a pair of sisters with painted brown hair, tiny bead eyes, closed mouth, and wearing matching muslin dresses, undergarments and dainty woven bonnets, one with a carved bone sewing basket; and doll with slightly-turned head, original wig, painted eyes and facial features, wearing blue cotton print dress with undergarments, woven pinafore to match the woven bonnet. Condition: generally excellent, some typical darkening of wax. Comments: English, mid-19th century. Value Points: very rare to find miniature wax dolls, especially notable as a sister pair and all three with fine original costumes. The dolls were featured in the book *Dolls in Miniature* by Evelyn Ackerman, page 56. $800/1200

3. German Bisque Lady with Sculpted Hair, with Cradle and Baby

8" (20 cm.) Bisque shoulder head with blonde sculpted hair in short curls, blue glass enamel inset eyes, painted features, closed mouth with primly-set lips, muslin body, bisque lower limbs, painted boots, wearing original costume. Condition: generally excellent, baby lacking one arm. Comments: Germany, circa 1880. Value Points: beautifully-sculpted hair and rarer glass eyes, included is an elaborate filigree soft metal hooded cradle with original gilt and ivory paint, and original bed fittings and taufling baby. $500/900

4. Beautiful French Bisque Block-Letter Bébé by Gaultier in Superb Original Costume

12" (30 cm.) Bisque socket head, amber brown glass paperweight inset eyes, dark eyeliner, painted lashes, feathered brows, rose-blushed eyeshadow, accented nostrils, closed mouth with accented lips, pierced ears, blonde mohair wig over cork pate, French composition and wooden eight-loose-ball-jointed body with straight wrists. Condition: generally excellent. Marks: F. 3 G. Comments: Gaultier, circa 1880. Value Points: very beautiful bébé with richly-decorated eyes, original body and body finish, wearing fine original ivory silk dress with matching Alencon lace borders and ivory silk faille sash, undergarments, socks, leather shoes, woven bonnet with velvet lining. $3000/4000

6. Six Early German Bisque Dollhouse Boys in Original Costumes and Presentation Box

3" (8 cm.) -5". Each has bisque or china shoulder head with sculpted short brown, black or blonde hair in boyish fashion, painted facial features, muslin body, bisque lower limbs. Condition: generally excellent. Comments: Germany, circa 1860s. Value Points: two with rare brown sculpted hair, each with original elaborately-detailed costumes, and presented in early glass-fronted presentation box. The dolls are shown and described "each is delicately fashioned to indicate his youthful attributes and handsome countenance" in *Dolls in Miniature* by Evelyn Ackerman, page 97. $700/1200

7. Pair, German Bisque Miniature Dolls as Aged Man and Woman

4 ½" (11 cm.) Each has bisque socket head, blue glass inset eyes, painted features, papier-mâché five-piece body with painted shoes, including aged man with long sculpted beard and moustache, pronounced nose, impressed age lines, original brown felt coat and black velvet cap; and aged woman with pronounced angular cheeks, chin and nose, closed mouth with gentle smile, wearing black silk costume with lace coiffe. Condition: generally excellent. Comments: Germany, circa 1890. The dolls are shown in Evelyn Ackerman's *Dolls in Miniature*, page 209, described as having "greatest detail of individual characterization". $600/900

5. Rare German Bisque Dollhouse Soldier with Original Costume and Sculpted Beard

7" (18 cm.) Bisque shoulder head depicting a mature man with defined age and worry lines and furrows, angular face, brown sculpted hair, thick brows, side-burns, bushy eyebrows, and long thick beard, painted blue downcast eyes, muslin body, bisque lower arms and legs with painted boots. Condition: generally excellent. Comments: Germany, circa 1890. Value Points: rare dollhouse model with superb sculpting, wearing original military costume with braid, cord, sash, medallions, epaulets, medals, helmet, and sword. The doll is featured in *Dolls in Miniature* by Evelyn Ackerman, page 235. $700/900

8. German Porcelain Boy in Fine Antique Costume

14" (36 cm.) Porcelain shoulder head depicting a young man, with slightly-pink-tinted complexion, black sculpted hair in side-parted fashion, painted blue eyes, red and black upper eyeliner, single stroke brows, closed mouth, muslin stitch-jointed body, leather arms. Condition: generally excellent, few original kiln specks on face, muslin body patched. Comments: Germany, circa 1870. Value Points: wearing black velvet fitted jacket with silver buttons, shirt, woolen trousers, brown leather ankle boots. $300/500

9. Rare 19th Century Panoramic Double-Sided Toy

6" (15 cm.) x 5". A firm-sided folio with marbled paper cover encloses an accordion-styled panorama with a different view on either side. One side features Solemn Ceremony (labeled in three languages on cover), and the other The Passing Across the Balcan (in three languages). Very good condition, some light fading. Very rare and beautifully designed early panoramic toy, mid-19th century. $600/800

10. German Bisque Dollhouse Soldier with Sculpted Beard and Original Costume

7" (18 cm.) Bisque shoulder head with sculpted light-brown hair, moustache and full beard, sculpted age furrows in face, painted blue downcast eyes, painted brows, muslin body with bisque lower limbs. Condition: generally excellent. Comments: Germany, circa 1890. Value Points: rare square-shaped beard and twirled moustache in rare color, wearing original military costume, cap and sword. The doll is shown in Evelyn Ackerman's *Dolls in Miniature*, page 236, described as having "a serious expression...implying a dedicated professional". $500/800

original blonde mohair wig with hip-length braids, peg-jointed slender arms and legs with painted white socks and black ankle boots. Condition: generally excellent, minor overpaint on upper left leg. Marks: 13 (arms and legs). Comments: French, circa 1882. Value Points: beautiful mignonette with expressive features, rare boots, wearing antique dotted Swiss dress with lace edging, woven bonnet, and along with six additional ensembles, chemise, and some accessories, with leather-covered wooden domed trunk. $900/1500

13. French All-Bisque Mignonette with Painted Blue Shoes

5" (13 cm.) Solid domed bisque socket head, blue glass enamel inset eyes, painted lashes and single stroke brows, accented nostrils, closed mouth with accented lips and hint of smile, blonde mohair wig, slender bisque torso, peg-jointed bisque arms and legs, painted white socks and blue two strap heeled shoes, original muslin chemise. Condition: generally excellent, chip at back upper edge of right leg. Comments: French, circa 1882, the dolls were presented as "poupées de poche" (pocket dolls) in the Paris Etrennes catalogs of that year. Value Points: an especially beautiful face with exquisite painting of features. $600/900

14. All-Bisque Mignonette in Lovely Silk Costume for the French Market

5" (13 cm.) Solid domed bisque swivel head on bisque torso, blue glass enamel inset eyes, painted delicate lashes and brows, accented

11. Pretty French Bisque Figure A Bébé by Jules Steiner in Original Dress

11" (28 cm.) Bisque socket head, blue glass paperweight inset eyes, painted lashes, brush-stroked and feathered brows, rose-blushed eye shadow, accented eye corners and nostrils, closed mouth with outlined lips, pierced ears, wheat-blonde mohair wig over Steiner pate, Steiner composition fully-jointed body. Condition: generally excellent, one finger reglued. Marks: J. Steiner Bte SGDG Paris Fre A 3 (head) (Steiner stamp on body). Comments: Jules Steiner, circa 1885. Value Points: very pretty shy bébé with lovely eyes and painting, original body and body finish, wearing original cotton print dress, undergarments, straw bonnet, red leather shoes and with red leather purse. $2500/3000

12. Wonderful French All-Bisque Mignonette with Trousseau and Trunk

6" (15 cm.) Solid domed bisque swivel head on elongated bisque torso, blue glass enamel inset eyes, painted curly lashes, feathered brows, accented nostrils, closed mouth with piquant smile, accent line between the lips,

nostrils, closed mouth with pert smile, blonde mohair wig, peg-jointed bisque arms and legs with painted white stockings and black two-strap shoes, wearing burgundy silk dress with lace edging and velvet bows, undergarments. Condition: generally excellent. Comments: for the French market, circa 1885. Value Points: very dear mignonette with most appealing charm. $400/600

15. Early Wooden Chest with Accessories

7" (18 cm.) l. chest. The mahogany three-drawer chest has gracefully-curved sides and front in the bombe fashion with ogee-shaped top, carved detail of dove-tailed drawers and wooden knobs, carved apron. Along with a pair of soft metal candelabras and a papier-mâché figure of jester in original costume. Mid-19th century. $400/600

16. Petite French Bisque Bébé Bru Jne, Size 0

9 ½" (24 cm.) Bisque swivel head with very full plump cheeks, on kid-edged bisque shoulder plate with modeled bosom and shoulder blades, amber brown glass paperweight inset eyes, feathered brows, outlined eye sockets, painted lashes, accented nostrils, closed mouth with accented lips, pierced ears, auburn mohair wig over cork pate, French kid bébé body with gusset-jointing at hips and knees, kid-over-wooden upper arms, bisque forearms, finely-costume in the original Bru manner with

antique fabrics, undergarments, socks, antique leather shoes and woven bonnet with maroon silk bows. Condition: generally excellent, bisque arms may be German bisque of the era. Marks: Bru Jne (and circle/dot imprint, on head) Bru Jne No. 0 shoulderplate. Comments: Leon Casimir Bru, circa 1880. Transitional model between the circle dot bébé which this closely resembles and the classic Bru Jne model with as this is marked. Value Points: charming bébé in very rare size, with sturdy body, dainty features. $6000/9000

17. Very Rare German Bisque Miniature Doll with Unique Bisque Sculpted Hat

8" (20 cm.) Bisque shoulder head with sculpted very tall shaded brown hat that is brush-stroked to suggest fur and decorated with black band, chin strap and red ornaments, with brown sculpted hair peeking at sides, painted brown eyes, black eyeliner, closed mouth, muslin body, bisque lower limbs, painted socks and black shoes, original undergarments. Condition: generally excellent. Comments: Germany, circa 1880. Value Points: very rare model, the doll is shown in Evelyn Ackerman's *Dolls in Miniature*, page 92, described as perhaps the only existing model and endowed with a "high state of artistic endeavor". $600/900

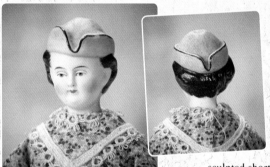

18. German Bisque Miniature Doll with Rare Lavender Cap

7" (18 cm.) Bisque shoulder head with sculpted purple cap having upturned edges and trimmed with black edging, darkest brown sculpted short curls, sculpted ears, painted facial features, blue eyes, muslin body, bisque lower limbs, cotton gown. Condition: generally excellent, very tiny flake at black edging may be original. Comments: Germany, circa 1880. Value Points: very rare model with exquisite detail of facial modeling, folds of bonnet, and stippling of hair. The doll is shown with detailed description in Evelyn Ackerman's *Dolls in Miniature*, page 92. $500/700

19. Early German Miniature Doll with Sculpted Bonnet and Original Costume

6" (15 cm.) Bisque shoulder head of adult lady with slender face, sculpted darkest brown hair drawn into ringlet curls at the back, sculpted yellow bonnet decorated with black band and a large purple lustre feather, painted facial features, muslin body, bisque lower limbs, black shoes. Condition: generally excellent. Comments: Germany, mid-1860s. Value Points: rare model with brown hair and fancy bonnet wears her original superb costume. The exquisite doll is shown in Evelyn Ackerman's *Dolls in Miniature*, page 172, described

19.

as "replete with costuming details, from the forward tilting bonnet to the extended crinoline skirt". $500/900

20. Extremely Rare German Bisque Doll with Sculpted Bonnet and Bellows Torso

6" (15 cm.) One-piece bisque head and upper torso, sculpted flat-top yellow bonnet with black edging and band decorated with a purple lustre feature, sculpted darkest-brown curly hair, painted blue eyes and facial features, muslin midriff enclosing (non-working) bellows, peg-jointed bisque arms, one-piece lower torso and plump legs with tiny ankles and feet, painted white

20.

socks with pink scallop trim, and purple lustre ankle boots. Condition: generally excellent. Comments: Germany, circa 1875. Value Points: very rare doll whose features include unusual construction, sculpted fancy bonnet, fancy boots, dark brown hair. $800/1200

21. Three Rare German Bisque Miniature Dolls with Sculpted Bonnets

7" (18 cm.) Each has bisque shoulder head with angular features of adult lady, sculpted hair and bonnet, painted facial features, muslin body, bisque lower arms, painted boots, and wearing original costumes. Condition: generally excellent. Comments: Germany, circa 1875. Value Points: the rare models are beautifully-preserved, each with very fancy and superbly-executed decorated bonnet; the two with lustre bonnets show decorative variations of the same model. The dolls are featured in Evelyn Ackerman's *Dolls*

21.

21 back view.

in Miniature, page 90 and 91 with special note by the author of the yellow bonnet lady whose bonnet is decorated by a hidden lustre plume at the crown and whose back bonnet ruffle is so realistically-modeled "that it seems possible to feel the fabric". $1500/2500

22. Four Tiny German Bisque Dolls with Sculpted Hats

3" (8 cm.) Each has bisque shoulder head with sculpted hair and decorative hat or coiffe, painted facial features, muslin body, bisque lower limbs, painted shoes, original costumes. Condition: excellent except purple lustre lady

22.

has restored shoulder plate, yellow bonnet has tiny flake on hat brim. Comments: Germany, circa 1875. Value Points: very rare models illustrate the variety of bonnet styles that were created, each with amazing detail of design and decoration. $600/1000

23. French Bisque Poupée with Rare Dehors Articulation, Elaborate Trousseau and Trunk

14" (36 cm.) Bisque swivel head on kid-edged bisque shoulderplate with Dehors deposed articulation allowing the head to tilt side-to-side and forward as well as swivel, cobalt blue glass enamel eyes, dark eyeliner, delicately-painted lashes and brows, accented nostrils and eye corncrs, closed mouth with outlined lips, ears pierced into head, blonde mohair wig over cork pate, French kid gusset-jointed body. Condition: generally excellent, body a tad weak. Comments: French, circa 1867, with rare Dehors articulation. Value Points: wearing a lovely antique ensemble comprising cotton print gown, undergarments, leather boots, and woven bonnet, the poupée also owns six additional antique gowns, five additional bonnets of various styles, bone-handled parasol, two additional pairs of boots (one pair signed C.C.), stockings, four pairs of gloves, corset and hoop, fan, brushes, jewelry and assorted sundries. $4000/6500

23 detail.

23 detail.

24. Rare French All-Bisque Mignonette in Original Brass Youpala and Bourrelet Cap

6" (15 cm.) Bisque swivel head on kid-edged bisque torso, cobalt blue glass eyes, painted features, single stroke brows, closed mouth with daintily-painted lips, blushed cheeks, blonde mohair wig over cork pate, peg-jointed bisque arms and legs, bare feet with over-painted (rubbed) shoes, wearing original costume. Condition: generally excellent, flake on left fingers. Comments: French, circa 1885. Value Points: the pretty mignonette is presented in original brass youpala (walker) with fitted stirrups for feet allowing the doll to "walk" when the youpala is moved forward; the learning-to-walk vignette is enhanced with original very rare woven miniature bourrelet cap and original dress. $1500/2000

25. An All-Original French All-Bisque Mignonette with Jointed Elbows

5" (13 cm.) Bisque swivel head on kid-edged slender bisque torso, cobalt blue glass enamel inset eyes, delicately-painted features and brows, accented nostrils, closed mouth with center accent lips, brunette mohair braids, peg-jointed shoulders and hips, bare feet, wooden ball-joints at elbows. Condition: generally excellent. Marks: BTE. Comments: French, circa 1880, the model is attributed to Schmitt et Fils. Value Points: very rare jointed elbow model with beautiful face is wearing her original ivory silk and lace costume and cap. $1200/1600

26. Pair, French Bronze Miniature Chairs with Attached Pets

5" (13 cm.) The cast bronze chairs in French salon style have embossed details and rich gilt finish. Mounted on each chair is a dog or cat, attached by hidden screw at the seat underside. Excellent condition. French, circa 1875, delightful miniatures perfectly scaled for display with mignonettes. $400/600

27. French Brown-Complexioned Bisque Poupée by Gaultier with Lovely Costume

16" (41 cm.) Ebony-black complexioned bisque swivel head on matching bisque shoulderplate, black enamel inset eyes, painted brows and lashes, closed mouth, pierced ears, black mohair wig over cork pate, brown kid gusset-jointed poupée body with stitched and separated fingers, wearing cotton print gown and undergarments. Condition: generally excellent. Marks: F. 3 G. (head and shoulders). Comments: Gaultier, circa 1878. Value Points: rare model whose rich complexion has a gleaming patina, original body, with rare accessories including bonnet, silk parasol, watch, lorgnette, boots. $2500/3500

28. French Wooden Miniature Furnishings in the Chinoiserie Style

16" (41 cm.) h. armoire. The two-piece set comprises a mirrored-front armoire and a three-drawer chest, each of maple wood, finished with black lacquer paint and decorated with gold leaf striping and decorations, along with colorful village and people scenes in the Chinoiserie style. Excellent condition, one wooden knob missing. French, circa 1890. $600/900

29. Very Beautiful and Rare French Bisque Bébé "H" by Halopeau in Fine Antique Costume

13" (33 cm.) Pressed bisque socket head with plump cheeks and chin, amber brown glass paperweight inset eyes, dark eyeliner, lushly-painted lashes, brush-stroked and multi-feathered brows, shaded nostrils, closed mouth with outlined lips, pierced ears, blonde mohair wig over cork pate, French composition and wooden fully-jointed body with straight wrists. Condition: generally excellent. Marks: 3/0 H. Comments: Halopeau, circa 1885. Value Points: an especially beautiful example of the rarely-found bébé with compelling presence, choicest bisque and painting, original body and body finish, and wearing fine white pique dress with soutache embroidered collar trimmed with cutwork, silk bonnet with ruffled frou-frou and lace, undergarments, cream kidskin ankle boots signed C.P. and gilt chain purse with cameo medallion. $18,000/30,000

30.

32.

31.

30. Two German Bisque Dollhouse Soldiers in Original Costumes

7" (18 cm.) Each has bisque shoulder head with painted brown hair, sculpted moustache, and painted facial features, muslin body, and bisque lower limbs. Condition: generally excellent. Comments: Germany, circa 1890. Value Points: the men have variations of sculpted moustaches, each wearing his factory-original costume and accessories. $600/900

31. Two German Bisque Miniature Dolls in Military Uniforms

4" (10 cm.) Including an all-bisque doll with sculpted black helmet decorated with a red plume, having sculpted brown hair and moustache, jointed arms and legs, painted boots, felt costume; and boy with socket head, painted features, five-piece paper mache body, and wearing original costume comprising helmet with gold decorations, and felt uniform. Condition: generally excellent. Comments: Germany, circa 1900. Value Points: rare sculpted helmet model with excellent detail of facial painting. $300/500

32. Two German Bisque Dollhouse Soldiers in Original Costumes

7" (18 cm.) Each has bisque shoulder head with sculpted short hair and curly moustache, painted facial features,

33.

muslin body, bisque lower limbs. Condition: generally excellent, costumes a tad faded. Comments: Germany, circa 1890. Value Points: the handsome moustache gentleman are wearing their factory-original costumes and swords. $500/800

33. Two German Bisque Dollhouse Gentlemen with Rare Moustaches and Hair Styles

7" (18 cm.) Each has bisque shoulder head with sculpted hair and beard, painted facial features, muslin body, bisque lower limbs with painted shoes, with cloth suit. Condition: generally excellent. Comments: Germany, circa 1890. Value Points: including gentleman with rare dark brown slicked-down hair and brown thick drooping moustache and goatee; and gentleman with comb-marked light brown hair, curly-tip moustache and very full beard. Both dolls are featured in Evelyn Ackerman's *Dolls in Miniature*, pages 244 and 245, described as "finely characterized". $500/800

34. Pair, German Bisque Miniature Dolls including Man with Sculpted Top Hat

6" (15 cm.) Each has bisque shoulder head with painted facial features, sculpted hair, muslin body, bisque lower limbs. Condition: generally excellent,

34.

35.

lady's left foot missing. Comments: Germany, circa 1880. Value Points: including gentleman with very rare sculpted top hat and well-defined sideburns, and lady whose fancily-designed hair is decorated with a black hair band, with original silk costume. $500/600

35. Two Rare German Bisque Dollhouse Gentlemen with Sculpted Beards

7" (18 cm.) Each has bisque shoulder head with sculpted hair and beard, painted features, muslin body, bisque lower limbs with painted shoes, antique costume including aged man with very long grey beard, full bushy moustache and neatly-arranged grey hair accented by piercing blue painted eyes; and man with light brown hair in off-center side part, having long sideburns, long curly moustache, and neat Vandyke beard. Condition: generally excellent, one foot missing. Comments: Germany, circa 1890. Value Points: very rare models, both dolls are featured in Ackerman's *Dolls in Miniature*, pages 245 and 246, described as "distinguished". $500/800

36.

37.

38.

36. Rare French All-Bisque Mignonette with Jointed Elbows and original Costume

5" (13 cm.) Bisque swivel head on kid-edged bisque slender torso, blue glass enamel inset eyes, long painted lashes, daintily-painted brows, accented nostrils, closed mouth with downcast lips, peg-jointing at shoulders and hips, wooden ball-joints at elbows, painted yellow ankle boots. Condition: generally excellent. Marks: BTE. Comments: French, attributed to Schmitt et Fils, circa 1882. Value Points: an especially appealing jointed-elbow model with rare boots, original muslin costume and bonnet. $1200/1600

37. French All-Bisque Mignonette with Beautifully-Shaped Limbs

5" (13 cm.) Bisque swivel head on kid-edged torso, slender neck, bright blue cobalt eyes, painted lashes, feathered brows, accented nostrils, closed mouth with center accent lines, blonde mohair wig, peg-jointed bisque arms and legs, bare feet. Condition:

generally excellent, tiny flake at left leg stringing hole. Comments: French, circa 1885. Value Points: rare model with lovely face and especially fine painting of features, beautifully-shaped limbs with tiny ankles. $500/800

38. French All-Bisque Mignonette with Bare Feet

5" (13 cm.) Bisque swivel head on kid-edged slender bisque torso, cobalt blue glass inset eyes, painted eye liner and charcoal eye shadow, single stroke brows, closed mouth with outlined lips, peg-jointed bisque arms and legs, bare feet. Condition: generally excellent. Marks: BTE. Comments: French, circa 1882. Value Points: unusual facial painting lends a highly-characterized look on the rare model. $600/900

39. Beautiful French All-Bisque Mignonette with Peach Boots

5" (13 cm.) Solid domed bisque swivel head on kid-edged bisque torso, large cobalt blue glass enamel inset eyes, dark eyeliner, painted lashes, feathered brows, accented nostrils, closed mouth with center accent line, blonde mohair wig in hip-length braids, painted white socks and peach ankle boots.

39.

Condition: generally excellent. Comments: French, circa 1885. Value Points: most charming shy smile enhanced by wide eyes, lovely complexion and rare boots. $600/800

40. Wonderful French Miniature Folding Room with Superb Original Furnishings

18" (46 cm.) l. 13"d. x 12"h. A firm-sided wooden box with decorative (faded) paper covers, forms into the floor of a five-sided room box; the room can be stored, when folded, neatly inside the box. The walls of the room have original papers with gilt beaded edging and there are glass windows at each side angle that are lavishly-covered with magenta silk draperies edged with self-ruffles, and having self silk ties, and lace inserts. Ornate ormolu mirrors are hung on the three other walls, and the room is furnished originally with silk upholstery and trim to match the draperies, including fireplace, piano, piano stool, fernery, settee, turtle-top pedestal table, and four chairs. An ornate ormolu clock with figural design sits on the mantel. Excellent unplayed with condition with vibrant colors and original finishes, so very rare to find in this condition. French, circa 1880. $2000/3000

41. Two French All-Bisque Mignonettes

5" (13 cm.) Each has bisque swivel head on kid-edged bisque torso, cobalt blue glass enamel inset eyes, painted features, closed mouth with prim lips, peg-jointed bisque arms and legs, bare feet, mohair wig, nice costume. Condition: generally excellent, brunette has chip at back upper torso. Comments: French, circa 1885. Value Points: charming pair of swivel head mignonettes with bare feet. $700/900

42 detail.

42. Beautiful French Porcelain Poupée by Madame Rohmer with Trousseau and Trunk

13" (33 cm.) Porcelain swivel head with flat-cut neck on original porcelain shoulder plate, the head and shoulder plate attached at crown according to Rohmer deposed system, very plump face, painted blue upper glancing eyes with shaded detail, large black pupils, black upper eyeliner with fringed detail,

42 detail.

feathered brows, accented nostrils and eye corners, closed mouth with accented lips, unpierced ears, plump body with gusset-jointing at hips, carved wooden lower legs, porcelain lower arms, original grommet-holes in torso designed for strings to place doll in seated pose (strings missing). Condition: generally excellent, very faint original firing line on lower left back shoulder plate, left thumb restored. Marks: Mme Rohmer Brevets. S.G.D.G. Paris. (stamp on torso). Comments: Madame Rohmer, circa 1863, the poupée has two deposed systems, the neck articulation and the seating system, by that dollmaker. Value Points: rare petite model with very beautiful expression and painting, the doll is

42.

presented with a lavish trousseau and trunk, which includes seven dresses, in addition to the costume she is wearing, four pairs of shoes, four bonnets, caps, bustle, bone-handled parasol, fans, five various purses, valises and boxes, miniature daguerrotypes, combs, brushes, and other various accessories. $3800/6500

43. All-Bisque Mignonette for the French Market

5" (13 cm.) Bisque swivel head on kid-edged bisque torso, cobalt blue glass eyes, painted lashes and brows, accented nostrils, closed mouth, blonde mohair wig, peg-jointed bisque arms and legs, painted white stockings and black two-strap shoes, nicely costumed. Condition: generally excellent. Comments: Germany, for the French market, circa 1890. Value Points: pretty wide-eyed child with pert smile. $500/700

44. Beautiful French Bisque Bébé Brevete, Size 2/0, by Leon Casimir Bru

14" (36 cm.) Pressed bisque swivel head with very plump cheeks and chin, on kid-edged bisque shoulder plate with modeled bosom and shoulderblades, brilliant blue glass enamel inset eyes with spiral threading, dark eyeliner, painted lashes, mauve-blushed eye shadow, lightly-feathered brows, accented eye corners, shaded nostrils, closed mouth with shaded and outlined lips, pierced ears, blonde mohair wig over cork pate, original kid gusset-jointed bébé body with square-cut collarette, bisque lower arms with sculpted fingers, lovely antique costume. Condition: generally excellent except restoration to three fingers of right hand. Marks: 2/0 (head) Bébé Brevete SGDG Paris (paper label on torso). Comments: Leon Casimir Bru, circa 1878, his first bébé model. Value Points: an especially beautiful model of the early bébé has gorgeous eyes, fine ivory-like complexion with subtle blushing that enhances the deeply-sculpted features, original signed body, carries antique bone rattle. $12,000/15,000

45.

45. German Wooden Dollhouse Furnishings with Lithographed Paper Designs

5" (13 cm.) h. cupboard. Each is of pinewood with lithographed paper overlay having elaborate designs to simulate carved and inlaid ebony, comprising cupboard with hutch top, cabinet with mirrored top, round pedestal table, sofa, and six side chairs. The sofa and six chairs have original red and black cotton fabric upholstery. Excellent condition. Germany, circa 1885. $400/600

46. German Wooden Dollhouse Furnishings with Lithographed Paper Designs

4 ½" (11 cm.) h. cupboard. Of pinewood with lithographed paper overlay to simulate carved oak with inlay designs and carvings, the set comprises a cupboard with front door, cabinet with mirrored top, additional mirror, oval pedestal table, round pedestal table, sofa, and six chairs. Very good condition, one chair leg missing, some wear on base of mirrored chest. Germany, circa 1885. $300/500

46.

47. German Wooden Dollhouse Furnishings for the French Market

5" (13 cm.) h. canopy bed. Of pinewood with carved detail, the furniture is decorated with applied gilt paper edging and trim, and includes a canopy bed with blue faille cover and canopy, mirrored front armoire and mirrored dressing table, each with blue chenille edging, and a fancily-shaped pedestal table. The furniture was made in Germany for the French market; its decorations and upholstery were the work of the French atelier of Victor Francis Bolant, circa 1890. $300/500

48. Three Petite German Porcelain Dolls in Original Costumes

3 ½" (9 cm.) Each has porcelain shoulder head with black sculpted hair, painted facial features, muslin body, porcelain lower limbs. Condition: generally excellent. Comments: Germany, circa 1875. Value Points: three various hair styles are included with wonderful detail of feathering, each doll with original costume. $300/500

49. Set of German Wooden Dollhouse Furnishings for the French Market, on Original Card

5 ½" (14 cm.) h. dressing table. Of pinewood, given a luxury touch with narrow gilt paper edging, and having original pale rose silk upholstery with lace and fringe trim, the set, still tied onto its original card, comprises canopy four poster bed, dressing table with mirror and canopy, another dressing table, oval pedestal table, stool, and four chairs. Excellent unplayed with condition. Made in Germany for the French market, upholstered and trimmed in the French atelier of Victor Francis Bolant, circa 1890. $400/600

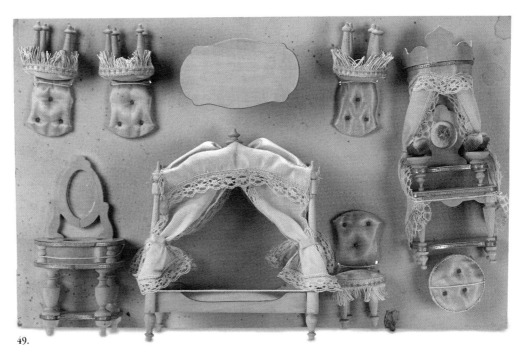

hands not original. Marks: Sie C 3/0 (and Steiner tiny red lettering at crown rim of head) Steiner 3/0 Bte SGDG (back of eyes). Comments: Jules Steiner, circa 1880. Value Points: most endearing beautiful early model with fine antique costume, bonnet, undergarments, original signed eyes. $2800/4000

50. Beautiful Petite French Bisque Bébé Steiner, Series C 3/0 with Signed Steiner Eyes

10" (25 cm.) Bisque socket head with rounded facial shape, blue glass sleep eyes that operate from wire lever at the back of head, painted lashes, brush-stroked and feathered brows, rose-blushed eye shadow, accented nostrils, closed mouth with outlined lips, pierced ears, blonde mohair wig in elaborate style, Steiner composition fully-jointed body. Condition: generally excellent, torso finish worn,

51. Collection of Rare German Ormolu Accessories by Erhard & Sohne

2 ½" (6 cm.) h. pedestal. Each of rich gilt ormolu with elaborate details, comprising pedestal, arm chair with upholstered seat, five various clocks including one with cherub figural in bronzed finish, pair of Art Nouveau vases, mirror on frame, three-arm candelabra, and wall-mounted candelabra. Very good/excellent condition. Germany, Erhard & Sohne, late-19th century. $400/700

52. French Miniature Baskets and Wooden Lidded Box

3" (8 cm.) h. barrel basket. Finely woven basket in tiny scale designs including a barrel-shaped hamper with hinged lid, two oval baskets with open-work sides, and a wooden box with carving on the lid. Excellent condition, rare to find, late-19th century. $200/400

53. Very Fine French Miniature Folding Room with Elaborate Decorations and Furnishings

21" (53 cm.) l. x 14"d. x 12"h. A firm-sided wooden box opens to serve as the floor and supporting walls for the five-sided walled room which can be stored folded within. When unfolded, the walls form an elegantly-fitted salon with richly-papered walls having defined moldings, paneling, and two floor-to-ceiling windows with fancily-decorated curtains. The box floor has tapestry-design paper finish to suggest carpeting. The room is fitted with luxury-quality rosewood and ebony furnishings including 11"h. armoire, 10"l. canopy bed, marble-top nightstand, faux-marble front fireplace, pedestal table and four bentwood chairs. The furniture is upholstered with blue silk comprising tufted seats, and fringed and braided borders, and the room is further decorated with a large gilt ormolu mantel mirror, two oval portraits in ormolu frames, very elegant mantel clock with figural designs, and candelabra. The room and furnishings are excellent, exterior box worn. French, circa 1875, an exceptionally luxurious room likely sold by prestige shop such as Maison Giroux. $3000/5000

54. Tiny French Bisque Bébé, Figure A, by Jules Steiner

8" (20 cm.) Bisque socket head, blue glass paperweight inset eyes, painted lashes and brows, accented nostrils, closed mouth with center accent line, pierced ears, blonde mohair wig over Steiner pate, Steiner composition fully-jointed body. Condition: generally excellent. Marks: Steiner Paris F A 1 (head) (original Steiner stamp on body). Comments: Jules Steiner, circa 1890. Value Points: most charming tiny size of the shy-faced bébé, wearing her original (dusty) silk dress. $1500/2000

55. Collection of 19th Century Accessories for Poupées

2" (5 cm.) l. workbaskets. Accessories and ephemera for French poupées or other lady dolls of the mid/late-19th century, including carved bone sewing basket, bone opera glasses, bone sewing case with tiny bone implements, bombe-shaped sewing case, leather sewing case, various other bone accessories, leather ankle boots marked "Modes de Paris", leather mule slippers marked "2", velvet and tulle bonnet, gloves, collar, fan, jewelry, and decorative hair combs. Very good/excellent condition. French, mid/late-19th century. $600/900

55.1. French Accessories for Poupées including "B" Shoes

4" (10 cm.) case. Including a firm-sided leather valise with gold pencil stripe and bail handle, fine woven bonnet with brown silk faille ribbons, feathers and trim, bone-handled parasol, leather purse, gloves, gilt album, and a pair of brown leather ankle boots (1 ¾"l.) impressed "1" and script letter "B". Excellent condition. French, circa 1870. $800/1200

56. German Porcelain Doll as "The Work-Table Companion"

Porcelain shoulder head with black sculpted hair drawn behind fully-sculpted ears, pink-tinted complexion, painted facial features, muslin body, porcelain lower limbs, painted black shoes. Condition: generally excellent. Comments: Germany, circa 1870. The doll is wearing her original costume laden with sewing ephemera including button trim around the skirt hem, pincushions, baskets, thimble, scissors, needles and more. A similar model was presented

in The Englishwoman's Magazine of that time named "The Work-Table Companion". Value Points: rare doll with wonderful accessories. $800/1000

57. Six Very Rare Miniature Dolls in Original Costumes and Boxes

3" (8 cm.) Each of the six dolls is shaped of a very fine kid or silk, with egg-shaped head that has minutely-painted facial features including details of stippled curls around the faces of the women, and painted beards or side burns on the men, firmly-shaped upper torso and arms, and with cork lower body designed to accommodate bristles. Condition: very good/excellent, bristles lacking. Comments: early-19th century, the miniature "bristle" or dancing dolls. Value Points: an extraordinary set of six dolls, the three pairs are preserved in their original boxes, and each is wearing a superbly-detailed original costume including stove-pipe hat and cravat on the gentlemen. The dolls were described in Ackerman's *Dolls in Miniature* book, page 47, with note made of the "individualized portraits". $400/600

58. Collection of Victorian Sewing Ephemera

6" (15 cm.) l. frame. Including a rosewood tapestry frame with bone tips, ebony-finished bentwood sewing box with velvet lining, carved bone pin-cushions with tape measure or spool bases, miniature lace bobbin, needle cases of various designs, and an amusing pup on a pillow with little paper message "I am a tape measure, pull my tail...". Very good/excellent condition. Mid/late-19th century. $600/900

59. Collection of Six German Miniature Sewing Machines

3" (8 cm.) -4"h. Of tin, soft metal or cast iron, the sewing machines are variously constructed, several designed with functioning treadles, one as penny toy, the soft metal models with richly painted finishes. Very good/excellent condition. Germany, late-19th/early-20th century. $300/500

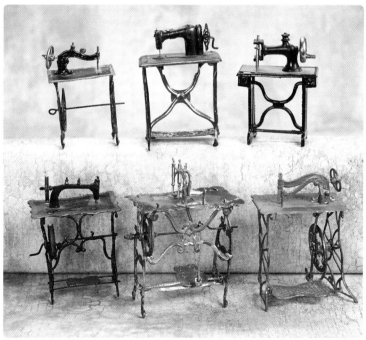

60. German Bisque Miniature Doll with Original Costume, with Dressing Table

5" (13 cm.) Bisque shoulder head with blonde sculpted hair, painted facial features, muslin body, bisque lower limbs. Condition: generally excellent. Comments: Germany, circa 1875, included is a fancy soft metal dressing table with mirror. Value Points: the lovely doll has large blue eyes, fancy hair with painted black snood edged with paper gilt flower, and wears her original gilt-trimmed green silk gown, and rare painted lavender shoes with painted side lacing. The doll is shown Ackerman's *Dolls in Miniature*, page 82. $400/500

61. Rare German Bisque Miniature Doll with Brown Hair and Original Costume

5" (13 cm.) Bisque shoulder head of slender-faced lady, brown sculpted hair waved smoothly around her face and captured in a modeled snood with pageboy curls, painted facial features, muslin body, bisque lower limbs, painted rose stocking ties, black shoes. Condition: generally excellent. Comments: German, circa 1870, included is a soft metal cabinet with attached gas lamp. Value Points: rarity factors include brown hair, fancy coiffure, and superb original costume decorated with tulle, gold braid, green paper leaves, and silk flowers. The doll is shown in Ackerman's *Dolls in Miniature*, page 80/81, described as "an elegant lady, stylish in every way". $500/700

62. German Bisque Lady with Brown Sculpted Hair in Original Costume

5" (13 cm.) Bisque shoulder head of slender-faced lady with very elaborate brown sculpted hair that is winged and braided at the front, and formed into a bead-trimmed chignon at the back, diminutive painted facial features, muslin body, bisque lower limbs, painted flat black shoes. Condition: generally excellent. Comments: Germany, circa 1870, included is a soft metal chest of drawers with attached mirror. Value Points: outstanding coiffure in rare brown color, the lady wears her original silk costume with braided trim. The doll is shown in Ackerman's *Dolls in Miniature*, page 84. $400/600

60-62 front.

60-62 back.

63. Two Rare Early German Bisque Miniature Dolls and Furnishings

4 ½" (11 cm.) Each of the dolls has a bisque shoulder head with blonde sculpted short curls, painted facial features, muslin body, bisque lower arms and legs, painted shoes. Condition: generally excellent. Comments: Germany, circa 1865, included is a set of lithographed-paper-over-wood doll house furnishing with original upholstery. Value Points: an exceptional pair of miniature dolls, each wearing its elaborate original costume trimmed with gold beading, paper edging, tinsel and lace. The dolls are shown in Evelyn Ackerman's *Dolls in Miniature*, page 82, described as "ornate confection". $700/1100

64. German All-Bisque Doll with Sculpted Hair by Simon and Halbig

4" (10 cm.) Bisque swivel head on kid-edged bisque torso, pale untinted bisque, brown sculpted hair in rolled curls behind the sculpted ears, black painted hair band, painted facial features, bright blue eyes, closed mouth peg-jointing at arms and legs, painted white stockings and grey ankle boots with black trim. Condition: generally excellent. Comments: Simon and Halbig, circa 1870. Value Points: rarity factors on the early model include brown hair, handband, and fancy boots. $300/500

65. Gorgeous German Bisque Lady with Lavender Hair Bow by Simon and Halbig, with Miniature Doll

13" (33 cm.) Bisque swivel head on kid-edged bisque shoulder plate, brown sculpted hair with two thickly-woven braids at the back of head centered by full curls and decorated by a sculpted lavender hair bow, blue glass inset eyes, dark eyeliner, painted lashes, feathered brows, accented nostrils and eye corners, closed mouth with piquant smile, center accent line on lips, ears pierced into head, original firmly-stuffed muslin body, bisque lower limbs, painted grey boots with black tips and buttons. Condition: restoration at the left lower throat (under velvet ribbon), otherwise excellent. Comments: Simon and Halbig, circa 1870. Value Points: gorgeous doll with rare brown hair and lavender ribbon, glass eyes, wearing fine antique costume over original body, and holding her own little all-bisque doll with sculpted hair, also by Simon and Halbig. $800/1100

66. Two German Bisque Dollhouse Men by Simon and Halbig

8" (20 cm.) larger. Each has bisque shoulder head with short brown sculpted wavy hair, painted facial features, blue eyes, black eyeliner, single stroke brows, closed mouth, muslin body, bisque lower limbs. Condition: generally excellent. Comments: Simon and Halbig, circa 1885. Value Points: each of the hard to find early dollhouse models is wearing his original costume. $400/600

67. Three German Bisque Miniature Dolls by Simon and Halbig

8" (20 cm.) largest. Each has bisque shoulder head, muslin body, bisque lower limbs with painted shoes; two have glass inset eyes, closed mouth, original mohair wigs with ringlet curls in the so-called rococo style, and the smaller has brown sculpted hair with hair band and painted facial features. Condition: generally excellent. Comments: Simon and Halbig, circa 1890. Value Points: well-preserved trio of miniature or dollhouse-sized dolls. $300/500

68. Petite German Bisque Closed Mouth Doll by Simon and Halbig with Her Own Doll

10" (25 cm.) Solid domed bisque shoulder head with very plump face, blue glass inset eyes, dark eyeliner, painted lashes, feathered brows, accented nostrils, closed mouth with center accent line, original commercial muslin stitch-jointed body with bisque lower arms, antique costume. Condition: generally excellent. Marks: S 2 H. Comments: Simon and Halbig, circa 1880. Value Points: rare early model with exquisite painting and most endearing expression, original body, holding her own little doll, chair is included. $800/1200

69. Petite Early German Bisque Doll by Simon and Halbig

6" (15 cm.) Solid domed bisque swivel head on kid-edged bisque shoulder plate, cobalt blue glass inset eyes, painted lashes, feathered brows, accented nostrils, closed mouth with slightly pouting expression, blonde fleeced hair, original muslin body with bisque lower arms and legs, bare feet, antique gown. Condition: generally excellent, left foot restored. Comments: Simon and Halbig, circa 1875. Value Points: rare early model with original body, little wooden chair is included. $400/500

70. Rare German Bisque Doll, 905, by Simon and Halbig

13" (33 cm.) Bisque swivel head on kid edged bisque shoulder plate, blue glass inset eyes, dark eyeliner, painted lashes, brush-stroked brows, accented nostrils and eye corners, closed mouth with center accent line, blonde mohair wig, kid gusset-jointed body, bisque lower arms, lovely antique costume. Condition: generally excellent. Marks: S 4 H 905 (head and shoulder plate). Comments: Simon and Halbig, circa 1875. Value Points: rare model with most endearing expression, finest quality bisque and painting, original sturdy body and superb antique costume. $900/1500

71. German Bisque Twill-Bodied Doll by Simon and Halbig

11" (28 cm.) Bisque swivel head on kid-edged bisque shoulder plate, bright blue glass enamel inset eyes, dark eyeliner, painted lashes, feathered brows, accented nostrils, closed mouth with hint of smile, accented lips, unpierced ears, blonde mohair wig, twill-wrapped body with dowel-jointing at shoulders, hips and knees, bisque lower arms, wearing antique lingerie and original kid sewn-on booties. Condition: generally excellent. Comments: Simon and Halbig, circa 1880, the doll was designed to compete with the French poupée, having shapely lady torso. Value Points: rare model with very beautiful face and well-designed body, original wig. $1500/2000

with outlined lips, pierced ears, blonde mohair wig over cork pate, Gesland body with composition shoulder plate and lower limbs, padded stockinette armature torso and upper limbs. Condition: generally excellent. Marks: F. 4 G. (head) (Gesland purple stamp on body). Comments: Gaultier, circa 1882, early block letter model and rare original body deposed by Pannier and created by Gesland. Value Points: the beautiful early bébé has lovely expression, rare body, superb antique costume, and owns her own pair of miniature bisque dolls with original costumes. $3500/4500

73. Three German Bisque Miniature Dolls and Ensemble of Gilt Soft Metal Furnishings

4 ½" (11 cm.) dolls. Each of the dolls has bisque shoulder head with sculpted hair and painted facial features, muslin body, bisque lower limbs. Condition: generally excellent, one foot tip broken. Comments: Germany, circa 1880. Value Points: rare coiffures including young boy and two ladies with superbly detailed coiffures, original costumes, along with an ensemble of gilded soft metal furnishings with elaborate forest scene designs including birds and deer. $500/800

74. Wonderful French Bisque Bébé "Lotte" by Leon Casimir Bru with Trunk and Trousseau

14" (36 cm.) Bisque swivel head on kid-edged bisque shoulder plate with modeled bosom and shoulderblades, brown glass paperweight inset eyes, dark eyeliner, painted lashes, brush-stroked and feathered brows, accented eye corners, shaded nostrils, closed mouth with outlined lips, pierced ears, ash-blonde mohair wig over

74 accessories.

72. Beautiful French Bisque Bébé with Gesland Body by Gaultier, with Tiny Dolls

14" (36 cm.) Bisque socket head with very plump face, brown glass paperweight inset eyes, dark eyeliner, painted lashes, widely-arched feathered brows, accented eye corners and nostrils, closed mouth cork pate, slender kid body with Chevrot-hinged hips and wooden lower legs, kid-over-wood upper arms, bisque forearms. Condition: generally excellent. Marks: Bru Jne 3 (head and shoulderplate) (Bru original paper label on torso). Comments: Leon Casimir Bru, circa 1885, included with the doll is an original miniature sepia photograph of the doll and a tiny red leather calling card case with calling cards having script written name "Lotte". Value Points: the beautiful brown-eyed bébé Lotte has original and perfect head, body and arms, and is wearing a lovely dress, bonnet, leather shoes, undergarments and stockings. Included is her antique trunk along with ten additional dresses (some fashioned of antique fabrics by Evelyn Ackerman and featured in her books, *My Favorite Patterns*), along with antique jewelry, bonnets, accessories, carriage blanket in leather straps, quilt, and leather bound miniature book with decoupage and original interior label "Henry Penny's Patent Metallic Books". $15,000/18,000

74 accessories.

75. Lavishly-Filled German Wooden Grocery and Novelty Store

29" (74 cm.) l. x 17"h. x 14"d. The wooden store features an open front flanked by two glass display windows that are ornamented with fancily-spindled columns, and side walls that angle outward for a feeling of spaciousness. The back wall has 12 spice drawers with original porcelain labels, a center display niche with mirrored back, and display niche at each end. There is a shelf above the back wall cabinets and a hanging shelf at one side; the other side features wooden wainscoting. A matching free-standing counter centers the store and there is original wall and floor paper throughout, as well as original exterior paint simulating stonework. The store contains a bounty of groceries, teas, a collection of miniature steins, trays of pastries, scale, rare figural gas lamp, three wooden dolls, and, curiously, hat stands with bonnets as though a milliner shop. Excellent condition. Germany, late-19th century. $2500/3500

76. Three Fine Early Grodnertal Wooden Dolls and Furnishings

6" (15 cm.) Each doll is all-wooden with one-piece head and shapely torso, elongated throat, painted hair with beautifully-detailed curls around the face, tiny painted facial features and cheek blush, two with original carved yellow tuck combs at crown, dowel-jointing at shoulders, elbows, hips and knees, painted shoes. Condition: generally excellent, tuck comb missing on one. Comments: Grodnertal, circa 1830. Value Points: rare early model with exquisite detail of painting that is wonderfully preserved, along with original detailed costumes. Included is a set of early wooden German dollhouse furnishings of the mid-19th century. $900/1200

77. Very Rare Pair of Grodnertal Wooden Tuck Comb Ladies with Original Costumes

9" (23 cm.) Each is all-wooden with one-piece head and torso, elongated throat, shapely bodice, carved wooden yellow tuck comb at the crown, painted black hair with shaded edging and exaggerated spit curls, original wooden earrings,

77.

78.

painted facial features and blush, dowel-jointing at shoulders, elbows, hips and knees, painted orange shoes. Condition: good, all original and un-restored, with some craquelure. Comments: Grodnertal, circa 1830, one of the pair is shown in Ackerman's *Dolls in Miniature*, page 33, described by the author as a "superior doll because both skilled craftsmanship and aesthetic considerations were part of what went into her creation". Value Points: the dolls have rare pierced ears with original yellow wooden earrings, and wearing matching gauzy costumes of unusual style, trimmed with gold ribbon and fringe. $900/1400

78. Two Grodnertal Wooden Dolls, Mother and Son, with Original Costumes

9" (23 cm.) Each is all-wooden with one-piece head and torso, dowel-jointing at shoulders, elbows, hips and knees, the woman with black painted hair decorated with highly-stylized spit curls and tuck comb, elongated throat, and tiny centered painted features; and the boy with short black hair, suggestion of sideburns, painted features. Condition: good, unrestored, costumes are original albeit frail. Comments: Grodnertal, circa 1830, the dolls were featured in Ackerman's *Dolls in Miniature*. Value Points: both dolls wear their original stylized costumes. $800/1100

79. Rare Grodnertal Wooden Gentleman in Original Costume

10" (25 cm.) One-piece carved wooden head and torso, unusual exaggeration of the heart-shaped elongated face, strongly-defined chin and broad forehead, painted black hair, painted facial features and complexion, stern expression, dowel-jointing at shoulders, elbows, hips and knees. Condition: original finish is well-preserved, rubs to hair at crown and back. Comments: Grodnertal, circa 1820, the doll is shown in Ackerman's *Dolls in Miniature*, page 33, described as a "splendid and rare specimen". Value Points: distinctive and compelling facial shape, the low-centered features enhancing the high brow, wearing his original gentleman's costume of the era. $400/600

79.

80. Eight Very Rare Early Miniature Wooden Dolls in Original Costumes

4" (10 cm.) Each has one-piece carved wooden head and torso, wooden limbs with cloth strip jointing, painted facial features and sculpted hair over gesso. Condition: generally excellent, some age wear to costumes. Comments: mid-19th century, the dolls were featured in a full chapter (pages 201-206) in Evelyn Ackerman's *Dolls in Miniature*, with noted similarity to a set of dolls then found in the Dingley Hall dollhouse of famous Bethnal Green Museum of Childhood. In that book, Evelyn Ackerman discusses the unique and special features of the dolls, noting the improbable, yet serendipitous, circumstance that the ensemble has remained intact, and offers possible attributions. Value Points: outstanding detail of individual hair styles, facial expression, and meticulous costume and accessories on the set of tiny dolls. $1200/2200

81. 19th Century Papier-Mâché Miniature Doll in Military Regalia with Gruber Signature

6" (15 cm.) Papier-mâché head and upper torso with sculpted grey beard, moustache and brows, sculpted green hat with extended black and gilt brim, painted facial features, firmly-stuffed muslin lower body, papier-mâché or wooden hands and feet, attached to original wooden

base. Condition: generally excellent. Marks: Clemens Gruber PuppenKonig Wien Graben 18 (and other illegible stampings). Comments: Gruber, who advertised himself as Puppenkonig or "king of dolls" offered costumed dolls from his Graben street shop in Vienna, late-19th/ early-20th century. Value Points: rare to find doll with maker's signature is well-preserved and is wearing his original well-detailed military costume and regalia. $400/600

82. German Wooden House with Christian Hacker Signature

27" (69 cm.) h. x 26"l. x 15"d. The wooden two-story house is created in three sections: two separate floors and a roof with delightfully painted second floor ceiling on the underside. The exterior of the house has original lithographed paper cover to simulate carvings and stonework, two large windows with elaborate wooden frames on each floor, and a wooden paneled door at the center of each floor, the bottom door with stenciled outlines and elaborate door knocker and knob, and the upper door fronted by a small balcony, and having a large glass window. The interior has two large rooms on the second floor with center opening door, and two rooms plus a center hallway with staircase on the first floor. The exterior papers and paint, and interior wall and floor papers and paint are original throughout. Structurally excellent, in as found condition, with faded and worn original papers and paint. The Christian Hacker paper label featuring intertwined CH letters and Schutzmarke are on the underside. Germany, Christian Hacker, late-19th century. $2500/3500

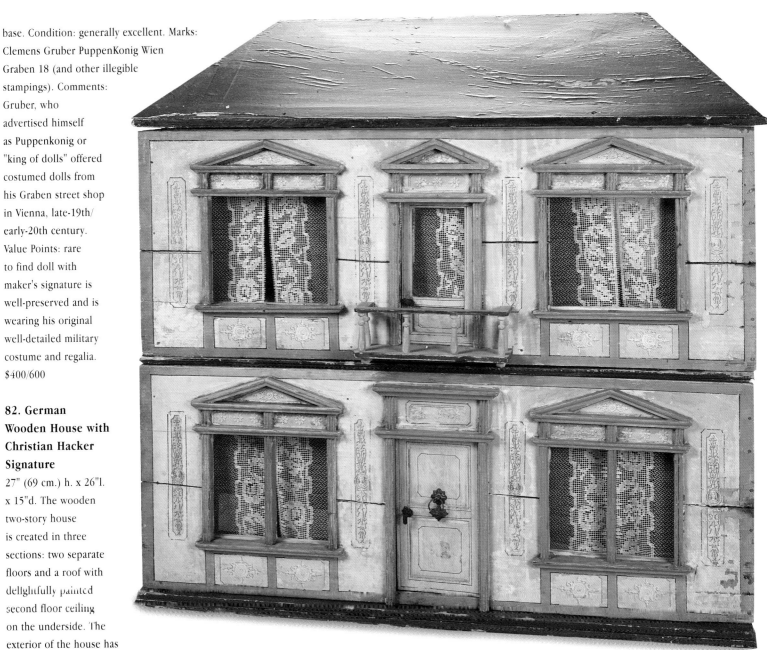

83. German Bisque "Nobbi Kid" by Marseille with Keywind Cymbals

8" (20 cm.) Bisque socket head, blue glass side-glancing googly eyes, painted lashes and brows, accented nostrils of tiny rounded nose, closed mouth with impish smile, blonde mohair wig, five-piece composition body, antique costume. Condition: generally excellent. Marks: A 253 M Nobbi Kid Germany US patd. Comments: Marseille, circa 1925, with internal mechanism which, when

85.

83, 84.

wound, causes the little googly to clap the cymbals he holds in his hands. Value Points: the googly has a cheerful countenance so suited to the rare activity. $400/600

84. German Toy Music Box Organ Grinder with Lithographed Decorations

11" (28 cm.) l. 9" h. The wooden music box contains a handwind mechanism within that creates tinkling street-organ music when the side handle is turned, and is decorated with lithographed papers in rich scroll and garland designs along with a scene of a street organ grinder and dancing children; with original tapestry over sound board, and canvas neck strap. Marks: a 678 (on paper at lower edge.) Condition: generally excellent. Comments: Germany, circa 1910. Value Points: rare and well-designed toy in well-preserved condition. $700/900

85. Collection of German Lithographed Tin Penny Toys

2 ½" (6 cm.) carriages. 6"h. bird cage pedestal. Each is of pressed tin with lithographed designs, including three various carriages (one with doll inside), tin "Doll's sulky", two various sewing machines, record player with gilt horn, child's high chair that reverses to become a play table, and a pedestal stand with birdcage. Excellent condition overall. Germany, early-20th century. $1000/1500

85.1. Three Miniature Books with Richly-Decorated Covers

2 ½" (6 cm.) Each of the books has embossed hard cover with gold lettering and design, and a decoupage accent, including *Susy Hall*, *Willie's Western Visit*, and *Dot's Travels*, each with interior illustrations and relating a short story about a child, published by the American Tract Society, 130 Nassau Street of New York, 1874. Excellent condition. $200/400

85.1.

87.

86. Delightful Ensemble of German All-Bisque Miniature Animals with Original Costumes

2" (5 cm.) -3". Each is all-bisque with painted animal fur or hide, characterized features, pin-jointed arms and legs. Condition: generally excellent. Comments: Germany, circa 1900, included are bear and tiny bear, piglet, and two bunnies. Value Points: rare to find, the animals are wearing factory-original knit costumes. $300/500

87. German All-Bisque Boy with Elaborate Original Costume and Pull Toy

4" (10 cm.) including hat. All-bisque doll has painted facial features, wig, pin-jointed bisque arms and legs, painted shoes and socks. Condition: generally excellent. Comments: Germany, circa 1900. Value Points: the little boy wears very elaborate folklore costume including top hat, and is pulling a wooden toy on wheels with die-cut figure of a rooster pulling a costumed bunny who is seated on a decorated egg, the toy marked Made in Germany. $300/500

86.

88.

88. German Bisque Laughing Child On Candy Container Bunny

9" (23 cm.) l. 11" h. A bisque-head doll with sculpted laughing expression and painted facial features, blonde mohair wig, carton torso, wooden lower arms and legs, painted shoes and stockings, is seated upon a fleece-covered papier-mâché bunny with glass eyes and removable head for use as a candy container. Condition: generally excellent. Marks: 13 a. Comments: Germany, circa 1900. Value Points: wonderfully-preserved condition of the rare candy container, with original costume and accessories. $800/1200

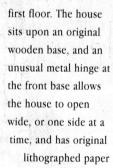

89. A Rare German Wood Dollhouse Featured on the Cover of *The Genius of Moritz Gottschalk* **by Evelyn Ackerman**

28" (71 cm.) h. (including chimneys) x 28"l. x 19"d. The wooden two story dollhouse is a confection of delightful architectural details from the high point of Victorian excess, known as "ginger bread trim". The front features a projecting center section with a second floor section that projects even further. The center is flanked by two front porches with set-in steps and, highly-carved columns and balustrades that lead to arched front windows and doors with carved frames. The porch roofs form into second-floor balconies with fancy balustrades, and there is an elaborate center gable with fretwork trim and two double-pot chimneys. Each side of the house has a projecting second floor gable window and elaborately framed arched windows on the first floor. The house sits upon an original wooden base, and an unusual metal hinge at the front base allows the house to open wide, or one side at a time, and has original lithographed paper cover to simulate yellow brick, and blue painted roof. The interior has two large and two small rooms with opening doors and a staircase with railing. The wall and floor papers are original and fancily designed with borders. Original curtains hang at all but two of the windows. As found condition, the house is wonderfully original albeit with worn and rubbed finish on paper and paint. Germany, Moritz Gottschalk, late-19th century, one of the most charming and fanciful creations by the firm, the house is featured on the cover of Ackerman's seminal book, *The Genius of Moritz Gottschalk*. $3500/5500

90. Erzebirge Wooden Mechanical Toy for the French Market

3 ½" (9 cm.) A wooden toy theatre with original painted blue frame and grey draperies has Punch and Judy figures posed upon the stage. When the lever at the side is pushed and pulled, Judy waves her stick at Punch and the two move to and fro. An original paper label on the base indicates the toy was sold at the luxury Parisian toy shop Au Paradis des Enfants. Excellent condition. Late-19th century. $400/500

91. Wonderful Vignette of Horse and Sleigh with Five All-Bisque Dolls

4" (10 cm.) Each of the five dolls has one-piece bisque head and torso, peg-jointed arms and legs, tiny glass inset eyes, closed mouth, painted features, mohair wig. Along with a soft metal winter sleigh and a hide-covered horse with original mane, harness, saddle and stirrups. Condition: generally excellent. Comments: Germany, circa 1900. Value Points: original factory costumes on each of the dolls, the soft metal sleigh is very rare. $800/1300

92. Two Miniature German Dolls with Wooden Swan Cart Toy

7" (18 cm.) l. coach. 6 ½" girl. An all-bisque girl with jointed arms and legs, mohair wig and glass eyes is seated in a wooden cart with two metal wheels, that is attached to a wooden swan on wheeled base. Standing alongside is a bisque shoulderhead boy with sculpted hair, painted features, muslin body, bisque limbs. Condition: generally excellent. Comments: Germany, circa 1900. Value Points: charming vignette, the swan cart is very rare and retains its original painted finish with details of swan feathers. $300/600

92.1. Three German Bisque Miniature Dolls in Original Regimental Costumes

5" (13 cm.) Each has bisque socket head, painted facial features, blonde mohair wig, five-piece composition body, painted boots. Condition: generally excellent. Comments: Germany, circa 1890. Value Points: each little boy is wearing a matching regimental costume of blue felt jacket with soutache cream braids, black short trousers, matching cap, and has little soft metal sword. $300/600

94. German All-Bisque Doll by Kestner

8" (20 cm.) Bisque swivel head on kid-edged bisque torso, brown glass sleep eyes, painted lashes and brows, open mouth, four tiny teeth, blonde mohair wig, peg-jointed bisque arms and legs, painted pink stockings and black one-strap shoes, pretty antique dress with embroidery, undergarments, bonnet. Condition: generally excellent. Marks: 40/10 (head and body) 10 limbs (limbs). Comments: Kestner, circa 1910. Value Points: larger size and swivel head. $300/500

93. German All-Bisque Doll with Two Soft Metal Canopy Cradles

6" (15 cm.) One-piece bisque head and torso, loop-jointed bisque arms and legs, brown glass eyes, closed mouth, painted features, original blonde mohair wig, wearing muslin night shift with lace trim. Condition: generally excellent. Marks: 150 2/0 (head) 2/0 (inside limbs). Comments: Kestner, circa 1910. Value Points: included is a matched pair of soft metal cradles with original ivory and gilt painting finish, canopy top with lace canopy, and original bed fittings, with tiny porcelain doll. $400/600

93.1. Rare Miniature German Porcelain Dishes

2 ½" (6 cm.) h. pot. Of fine white porcelain the service features teapot, creamer and sugar styled in figural designs of seated Chinese man with colorful costume and moustache; the sugar bowl features a lid in the shape of traditional cap. The service includes two creamers, lidded sugar, three cups and saucers. Excellent condition. Germany, circa 1890. $200/400

95. Early German All-Bisque Doll by Kestner with Baby Carriage

6" (15 cm.) Bisque swivel head on kid-edged bisque shoulderplate, brown glass sleep eyes, painted features, closed mouth, blonde mohair wig with long looped braid over plaster pate, peg-jointed bisque arms and legs, painted blue ankle boots with magenta tassels, silk dress. Condition: generally excellent. Marks: 0 (head, torso, arms). Comments: Kestner, circa 1880. Value Points: rare early swivel head model with original wig, rare painting of boots, along with a soft metal baby carriage with original gilt accents. $800/1000

96.

96. Rare German Bisque Miniature Doll by Kestner with Seldom Found Body

7" (18 cm.) Bisque swivel head on kid-edged bisque shoulder plate, blue glass sleep eyes, painted lashes, feathered brows, accented nostrils and eye corners, closed mouth with center accent line, blonde mohair wig in hip-length braid over plaster pate, peg-jointed bisque arms, kid lower torso and legs with gusset-jointing at hips and knees. Condition: generally excellent. Marks: 2 ½ (head, torso and arms). Comments: Kestner, circa 1885, the doll was inspired by the kid body of the Bru bébé. Value Points: very rare miniature model by Kestner with original sturdy body, wig, pate, and beautiful expression and bisque. $1100/1500

97. German Bisque Closed Mouth Child by Kestner

15" (38 cm.) Bisque socket head, brown glass sleep eyes, painted lashes, brush-stroked and feathered brows, accented nostrils and eye corners, closed mouth with accent line between the lips, blonde mohair wig over plaster pate, composition and wooden eight-loose-ball-jointed body with straight wrists, fine antique costume and leather shoes. Condition: generally excellent. Marks: 10. Comments: Kestner, circa 1885. Value Points: beautiful child model with endearing pensive expression, fine quality bisque and painting, original early body and body finish $1200/1600

99. French Wooden Wash Table and Accessories

7" (18 cm.) h. The ebony-finished wooden washing table has fancily-spindled legs, and cut-out table top for insertion of wash bowl. Included is porcelain wash bowl and pitcher with blue and black accents, and various accessories including comb, chatelaine, basket. Excellent condition. French, circa 1885. $200/400

100. French Porcelain Toilette Service for Poupée in Original Box by CBG

10" (25 cm.) l. box. The firm-sided box with original paper covers and oval medallion lettered "Toilette C.B.G. Paris" opens to reveal a rose paper lined interior, mirrored back, and porcelain toilette service and accessories, still tied to original base. The toilette set, of white porcelain background is decorated with borders of blue and gilt with dainty floral trim, and comprises wash bowl and pitcher, jar and five various lidded containers, along with brushes, mirror, combs, cologne bottle. Excellent condition. French, Cuperly, Blondel and Giroux, circa 1885. $600/900

98. Petite French Bisque Bébé Jumeau with Original Body

10" (25 cm.) Bisque socket head, blue glass paperweight inset eyes, painted lashes, dark eyeliner, brush-stroked brows, accented nostrils, closed mouth with outlined and shaded lips, pierced ears, brunette mohair wig over cork pate, French composition and wooden fully-jointed body, with antique silk and beaded baby bonnet, and antique undergarments. Condition: generally excellent. Marks: (faint Jumeau red stamp on untinted square at back of head). Comments: Emile Jumeau, circa 1892, Bébé Reclame, created under commission for various Parisian department stores of the era such as Au Bon Marche and Samaritaine. Value Points: wonderful petite size with deep paperweight eyes, original body in near mint condition. $2500/3500

101. Outstanding French Bisque Bébé by Adelaide Huret with All-Wooden Articulated Body

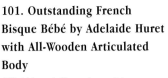

18" (46 cm.) Very plump bisque socket head with classic light-bulb shaped throat, very full cheeks and chin, pale complexion with delicately-tinted blush on cheeks, chin and brows, small blue glass enamel inset eyes with spiral threading, dark eyeliner, delicately-painted brows and lashes, accented nostrils, tiny closed mouth with outlined lips, un-pierced ears, ash-blonde mohair wig over cork pate, all-wooden body with shapely torso, dowel-jointing at shoulders, elbows, wrists, hips, knees and ankles, separately-carved fingers. Condition: generally excellent, body is professionally repainted. Comments: Huret, circa 1879, the Bébé Huret was created under the supervision of Adelaide Huret who had been inspired by the "new" style of doll, the bébé, introduced by others at the 1878 Universal Exposition in Paris. The Bébé Huret was fitted with a child-proportioned body made of gutta percha or (as in this case) a fully-articulated wooden body in the style of Bru's Bébé Modele, and with painted eyes or (as in this case) with glass enamel eyes. Value Points: the pale complexion of the very beautiful bébé contrasts superbly with the plumply-modeled features; the bébé is rarely found, and wears a very fine original pique and embroidered costume, undergarments, silk bonnet, leather shoes with silk rosettes, and carries kidskin gloves and a peach silk parasol. $15,000/18,000

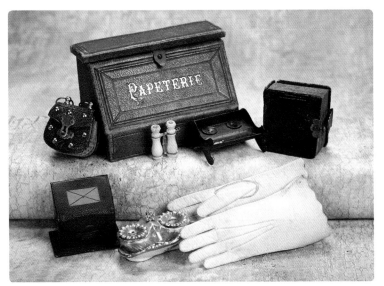

103. 19th Century Writing Accessories for Poupée or Small Bébé
4" (10 cm.) l. papeterie. Including firm-sided French Papeterie with brown-leather cover and gold lettered word, that hinges open to form a writing desk and is filled with various bone writing tools and stationery; along with a green leather envelope box, porcelain double-inkwell, miniature leather album filled with tiny tintypes, cream leather gloves, bone opera glasses, leather purse (strap broken) and a rare painted tin double inkwell with gold stenciled trim. Excellent condition overall. Mid/late-19th century, mostly French, the album in English. A wonderful collection of miniature accessories. $600/900

102. Tiny French Bisque Early Model Bébé by Jules Steiner
10" (25 cm.) Bisque socket head with plump rounded face, pale complexion, blue enamel inset eyes, dark eyeliner, painted lashes and feathered brows, closed mouth with accent line between the lips, pierced ears, ash blonde mohair wig, cork pate, Steiner composition fully-jointed body, lovely antique costume. Condition: faint hairline from left side of forehead to left eye. Marks: 3/0. Comments: Jules Steiner, circa 1877. Value Points: rare early period bébé in enchanting size. $1800/2300

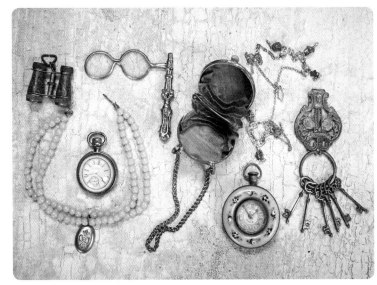

104. 19th Century Miniature Doll Jewelry

3" (8 cm.) overall length chatelaine. Including soft metal chatelaine with belt loop and five keys, turquoise watch with painted enamel finish that is marked H.H. Paris, turquoise beads with gold medallion drop, gold-plated watch, leather-wrapped brass opera glasses, gold lorgnette, gold chain necklace with coral drops, and a gold-plated purse with blue silk lining. Excellent condition. A wonderful collection in traditional mid/late-19th century designs and colors. French, circa 1870/1890. $300/600

105. Pair of French Doll Chairs with Rare Aqua Tufted Seats

11" (28 cm.) Of fine maple wood with natural finish, in faux-bamboo style carvings, the pair of chairs feature spindle backs and front legs, and have original seat covers of aqua silk with matching braid fringe and deep tufting with self-covered buttons. Excellent condition. French, circa 1880. (Note only one chair shown in photograph). $400/700

106. Beautiful French Bisque Bébé by Schmitt and Fils in Fine Antique Costume

13" (33 cm.) Bisque socket head with pear-shaped modeling, very full cheeks, blue glass enamel inset eyes with spiral threading, dark eyeliner, painted lashes, feathered and fringed brows, rose-blushed eye shadow, accented eye corners and nostrils, closed mouth with outlined lips, pierced ears, blonde mohair wig over cork pate, French composition and wooden eight-loose-ball-jointed body with straight wrists and flat-cut derriere. Condition: generally excellent, slight nose tip rub. Marks: Sch (in shield with crossed swords, on head and derriere) 00 (head). Comments: Schmitt et Fils, circa 1882. Value Points: lovely size of the sought-after bébé, with original signed body, wearing gorgeous antique costume and bonnet. $7000/9500

107. Beautiful Early French Bisque Poupée with Dehors Articulation and Cobalt Blue Eyes

17" (43 cm.) Bisque swivel head on kid-edged bisque shoulder plate, luxury neck articulation allowing the head to tilt side-to-side and forward as well as swivel, brilliant cobalt blue glass enamel inset eyes, thick dark eyeliner, painted lashes, feathered brows, accented nostrils and eye corners, closed mouth with outlined lips, ears pierced into head, brunette human hair wig over cork pate, French kid gusset-jointed body with shapely torso, stitched and separated fingers. Condition: generally excellent, tiny flake at neck edge of back shoulder plate. Comments: French, circa 1867, with Dehors deposed neck articulation system. Value Points: compelling presence of the poupée achieved by brilliant eyes, realistic head posturing and superb antique silk gown with black Alencon lace, velvet and lace bonnet, earrings, undergarments, stockings and heeled ankle boots. $2200/2700

108. French Bisque Bébé Jumeau, Incised Depose Model, Size 4 with Signed Jumeau Shoes

13" (33 cm.) Bisque socket head, deep blue glass paperweight inset eyes, dark eyeliner, lushly-painted lashes, brush-stroked and feathered brows, rose-blushed eye shadow, accented nostrils, closed mouth with outlined lips, pierced ears, blonde mohair wig over cork pate, French composition and wooden fully-jointed body with straight wrists. Condition: generally excellent. Marks: Depose Jumeau 4 (incised) Jumeau Medaille d'Or Paris (torso). Comments: Emile Jumeau, circa 1884, the model was made for one year only. Value Points: an especially pretty shy-faced bébé with deep blue eyes, lovely complexion, original body and body finish, wearing antique white dress with lace and tucks, undergarments, blue velvet bonnet, Jumeau socks and signed Jumeau shoes. $3000/4000

109. Rare First Period French Bisque Bébé E.J., Size 1

11" (28 cm.) Pressed bisque socket head with very full lower face, blue glass enamel inset eyes in hand-cut eye sockets, painted lashes, feathered brows, closed mouth with outlined lips, dimpled chin, pierced ears, blonde mohair wig over cork pate, French composition and wooden eight-loose-ball-jointed body with straight wrists, wearing pretty early costume, undergarments, socks, leather shoes. Condition: irregular cut at left eye corner (original or flake?), left cheek rub, original body and body finish albeit somewhat worn. Marks: 1 EJ. Comments: earliest period of the signature E.J. bébé, this example more closely resembles the very first Jumeau bébé known as "premiere", circa 1881. Value Points: rare model with endearing shy expression. $2500/3200

110. Wonderful Ensemble of French Diminutive Doll Furnishings

11" (28 cm.) h. armoire, 6 ½" h. chairs. Of pine wood, with original aqua painted finish, the seven-piece ensemble comprises bed with original silk fittings, marble top wash stand and night table, table, mirrored-front armoire, and two fancily-spindled chairs with tufted silk seats and braid edging. Excellent condition. French, circa 1880, a luxury and rare set in unusual diminutive size is wonderfully-preserved. $800/1000

111.

112.

113.

111. German Bisque Dollhouse Dolls as Bride and Groom

7" (18 cm.) Each has bisque shoulder head, glass eyes, painted features, muslin body, bisque lower limbs, painted shoes, she with mohair wig, slender throat, and wearing her factory original (silk worn away) lavish lace wedding gown with veil and flowers, and he in formal suit with sculpted brown center-parted hair and moustache. Condition: generally excellent. Comments: Germany, circa 1890. Value Points: lovely couple with glass eyes, original costumes. $600/900

112. Three German Glass-Eyed Bisque Dollhouse Dolls with Salon Furnishings

6" (15 cm.) and 7". Each doll has bisque shoulder head with glass inset eyes, closed mouth, painted features, muslin body, bisque lower limb and antique costume; including two women with original mohair wigs, marked SH 1160; and a gentleman with sculpted hair and modeled moustache, in factory-original formal evening wear suit. Condition: generally excellent. Comments: Germany, circa 1890. Value Points: hard-to-find models, included is a three-piece set of salon furnishings including marble top table. $400/700

113. Collection, Twelve German Ormolu Miniature Accessories by Erhard and Sohne

2 ½" (6 cm.) h. figural clock. Each is of richly-gilded ormolu with embossed or raised designs, including fireplace hod for coal or wood, fireplace fender, plant stand, two various umbrella stands, fancily-framed print of child placing a bonnet on her pup's head, mirror stand (no mirror), candle holder with ebony figural, three-part desk photograph frame with two original celluloid images, fancy candle holder, footed fruit dish, and a fine mantel clock with porcelain clock face and figural design of man with cape and horn. Excellent condition. Germany, Erhard & Sohne, end-19th century. $700/1100

114. Three German Bisque Dollhouse People with Rare Features

7" (18 cm.) Each has bisque shoulder head with sculpted hair, glass eyes, painted features, muslin body, bisque lower limbs, and is wearing antique or original costume. Condition: generally excellent. Comments: Germany, circa 1890. Value Points: having rare glass eyes, the man with rare dark brown hair, moustache and goatee, and the adult woman with fancy chignon. $600/900

115. German Wooden Dollhouse Furnishings

7" (18 cm.) h. desk. The rosewood-finished upright desk in the Empire tradition has drop front with green paper lining, interior drawers, one upper drawer and two lower drawers and is trimmed with ivory-painted columns and edging. Along with four salon chairs with gilt stenciling and original velvet-upholstered seats. Excellent condition. Germany, Walterhausen, circa 1885. $300/600

114, 115.

116. Rare German Bisque Dollhouse Lady with Sculpted Torso

5 ½" (14 cm.) One-piece bisque head, torso, upper legs and upper arms with sculpted and painted details of corset, sculpted short black curly hair, painted facial features, muslin mid-arms and mid-legs, bisque lower

116.

arms and leg. Condition: hairline across the front shoulder plate, some bisque spotting. Comments: Germany, circa 1870. Value Points: very rare model. $300/500

117. Four German Bisque Flapper Dollhouse Ladies with Jointed Arms

6" (15 cm.) and 7". Each has solid domed bisque shoulder head to midriff, pin-jointed arms in bent pose, very angular shape of face, painted features, mohair wig, muslin body,

117.

bisque lower limbs with painted stockings, shoes or boots, antique or original costumes. Condition: generally excellent. Comments: Germany, circa 1915. Value Points: rare to find flapper era ladies with stylized posing and costumes. $500/900

118.

118. Three German Black-Complexioned Bisque Dollhouse Dolls

5" (13 cm.), 7, and 8". Each is bisque shoulder head with ebony black complexion and sculpted hair, painted facial features, muslin body, black bisque lower limbs. Condition: generally excellent, woman missing right foot. Comments: Germany, circa 1890. Value Points: rare models, each wearing factory-original or antique costume, the gentleman particularly handsome with matte bisque complexion, and glazed finish on hair. $500/900

120. German Bisque Dollhouse Lady "Automobilfahrerin" in Original Box and Costume

5" (13 cm.) Bisque shoulder head lady with sculpted blonde hair in chignon, painted facial features, muslin body, bisque lower limbs, painted shoes and socks. Condition: generally excellent. Comments: Germany, circa 1910. Value Points: wearing her factory-original costume of dress, undergarments, plush coat, hat with veil, and handbag, the lady is presented in her original box labeled "Automobilfanrerin" (motorcar passenger). $500/700

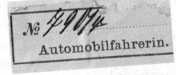

№ 79074
Automobilfahrerin.

119.

119. Three German Bisque Dollhouse Men with Sculpted Hats

5" (13 cm.) and 6". Each has bisque shoulder head with sculpted hat, painted facial features, muslin body, bisque lower limbs, and painted shoes. Condition: generally excellent. Comments: Germany, circa 1900. Included is man with moustache with formal top hat, business man with black rounded-top derby, and business man with black-banded grey hat, each with factory-original costume that is compatible to his hat. $600/900

121. Four German Bisque Dollhouse People as Chauffeurs or Aviators

3" (8 cm.) -5". The larger two have bisque shoulder head with sculpted cap to represent its occupation, the aviator with goggles pushed up onto helmet, and the chauffeur with driving glasses, each with painted features, muslin body, bisque lower limbs. The smaller two are all-bisque with jointed limbs, and painted boots or stockings, she with aviator cap and goggles and he with chauffeur's cap. Condition: generally excellent. Comments: Germany, circa 1910. Value Points: rare

121.

occupational models with distinctive features, each in factory-original costume. $7800/1200

122.

122. Three German Bisque Dollhouse Men as Golfers

5" (13 cm.) largest. Each has bisque shoulder head with sculpted and painted golfer's cap, painted features, muslin body, bisque lower limbs, painted knee-high leggsing and

shoes, and is wearing original golfer's costume, three slightly larger golf clubs included. Condition: generally excellent. Comments: Germany, circa 1900. Value Points: rare models, each wearing factory original costume, the larger with especially fine detail of painting on cap and leggings. $500/700

123. Three German Bisque Dollhouse Men with Sculpted Caps

6" (15 cm.) Each has

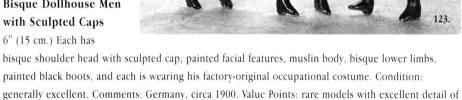

123.

bisque shoulder head with sculpted cap, painted facial features, muslin body, bisque lower limbs, painted black boots, and each is wearing his factory-original occupational costume. Condition: generally excellent. Comments: Germany, circa 1900. Value Points: rare models with excellent detail of cap sculpting and painting, the gent with black-brimmed cap also has modeled moustache. $600/900

124. Four German Bisque Dollhouse Soldiers with Moustache, in Original Regimental Uniforms

6" (15 cm.) and 7". Each has bisque shoulder head with sculpted hair and moustache, painted facial features, muslin body, bisque lower limbs, painted shoes. Condition: generally excellent. Comments:

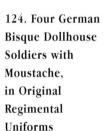

124.

Germany, circa 1890. Value Points: each is wearing factory-original different regimental costume with accessories, all with sculpted moustache and three with rarer brown eyes. $600/900

125. English Poured Wax Child Doll in Original Costume

15" (38 cm.) Poured wax shoulder head with inset cobalt blue enamel eyes, painted features, closed mouth, brunette mohair inserted hair, softly-stuffed muslin body with poured wax lower limbs, bare feet. Condition: overall good, painted of facial features is faded. Comments: English, possibly Montanari, circa 1880. Value Points: the little doll wears her original (frail) mauve silk gown and matching cap with lace and crystal bead trim, silk ribbons, matching cap, undergarments, stockings, and shoes. $500/800

126. Two Early French Mechanical Toys with Bisque Dolls by Vichy

10" (25 cm.) Each is a bisque head doll with large blue glass enamel eyes, painted features, closed mouth, mohair wig, on firm carton body and legs, with metal hands, standing upon a three-wheeled tinplate platform which, when wound, causes the doll to glide forward and move in circles, all the while turning its head and waving its arms up and down. Condition: generally excellent, costumes are original albeit frail. Comments: Vichy, circa 1865. Value Points: the delightful luxury toys include a young lady and young lad in original Louis XVI style costumes, she with garland of flowers and he with grapes and vines. $3000/5000

127. Petite French Bisque Poupée by Gaultier, Size 3/0

9" (23 cm.) Bisque swivel head on kid-edged bisque shoulder plate, blue glass enamel inset eyes, painted lashes and brows, closed mouth, pierced ears, blonde mohair wig, kid poupée body with gusset-jointing at knees and elbows, lovely silk costume, undergarments, antique bonnet and shoes. Condition: Generally

excellent. Marks: F.G. (shoulder plate 3/0 (head and Shoulder plate). Comments: Gaultier, circa 1875. Value Points: rare diminutive size with signed head and shoulders. $900/1200

128. Petite French Bisque Poupée in Original Costume, Size 4/0

10" (25 cm.) Bisque swivel head on kid-edged bisque shoulder plate, blue glass inset eyes, painted lashes and brows, closed mouth with tiny lips, pierced ears, brunette mohair wig over cork pate, French kid slender poupée body. Condition: generally excellent. Marks: 4/0 (head) 0 (and) 4 (shoulders). Comments: French, circa 1880. Value Points: the tiny Parisienne wears her

original red cotton frock with ivory inset panel, undergarments, black shoes, lovely woven bonnet. $800/1100

129. French Maple Wood Armoire with Mirrored Front

23" (58 cm.) The maple wooden armoire features a mirrored front door with faux-bamboo framing that is repeated at the crown and side columns, and centers unusual marbled maple veneers; with finial ornaments at the two front corners, and lock and key. Excellent condition. French, circa 1885. $300/500

130. French Bisque Poupée by Jumeau with Signed Jumeau Body

18" (46 cm.) Bisque swivel head on kid-edged bisque shoulder plate, blue glass enamel inset eyes with spiral threading and dark blue outer rims, dark eyeliner, painted lashes and brows, accented nostrils, closed mouth with outlined lips, pierced ears, brunette mohair wig over cork pate, French kid poupée body with gusset-jointing, stitched and separated fingers, maroon silk costume, undergarments, fringed velvet cape, wonderful antique shoes. Condition: generally excellent, body a tad weak. Marks: 6 (head). Jumeau Medaille d'Or Paris (body stamp). Comments: Emile Jumeau, circa 1880. Value Points: lovely gentle expression and signed original body. $2000/2500

131. Outstanding Set of Mid-19th Century Wooden Dollhouse Furnishings

8" (20 cm.) desk. Of fine wood, possibly cherry, with inlay designs on several pieces, the fine 14-piece ensemble includes a large round pedestal table with tripod feet, a smaller pedestal table, three drawer chest (one knob missing), glass front bookcase with original green paper lining, hall floor-length mirror, sofa with original rose silk upholstery and gilt paper edging, unusual drop leaf parlor table, desk with sunray design on the drop front that opens to a writing surface and interior niches, and a set of six side chairs with unusual curved construction of the backs and original rose silk upholstery with gold paper edging. Excellent condition. Of exceptional maitrise-quality workmanship, and beautifully-preserved with original finishes. Continental, mid-19th century. $1200/1700

132. A Family of Grodnertal Wooden Dolls and Furnishings

4" (10 cm.) -7". Each of the five dolls is all-carved wood, with one piece head and torso, dowel-jointing of shoulders, elbows, hips and knees, and having carved painted black hair with delicately feathered or ringlet curls around the face, and three with yellow tuck combs, dowel-jointing at shoulders, elbows, hips and knees, painted shoes. Condition: generally excellent, doll with lacy costume is missing one leg. Comments: Germany, early/mid-19th century. Value Points: wonderful group of early Grodnertal dolls, with well-preserved original painting, and wearing original costumes; included is a four piece set of wooden miniature furnishings with colorful decoupage decorations. $900/1300

133. Two Early Grodnertal Dolls with Rare Hair Styles

4 ½" (11 cm.) and 7". Each is all-carved wood with one-piece head and torso, sculpted hair and painted facial features over ivory complexion, with pin and

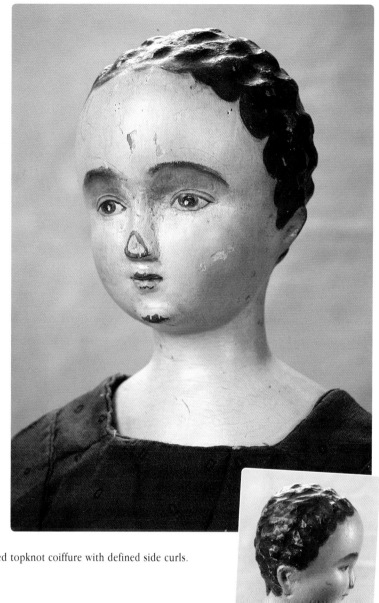

dowel jointing at shoulders, elbows, hips and knees, painted shoes. Condition: generally excellent, one foot front missing on each doll. Comments: Grodnertal, early-19th century. Value Points: the larger doll has especially notable shape of upper torso designed to accommodate fashions of its era, and rare carved topknot coiffure with defined side curls. $500/800

134. Compelling Early Carved Wooden Doll

26" (66 cm.) Carved wooden shoulder head with elongated throat and artistically-carved head and hair, with scalloped curls framing the face and tucked behind sculpted ears, then overall wavy curls at the back, sculpting detail of the face includes defined eye sockets, nose, mouth, and chin, painted detail of features includes brown downcast eyes with white eyedots, red and black upper eyeliner, ochre- blushed eye shadow, feathered brows, closed mouth, original hand-stitched muslin body with leather hands. Condition: nose tip chipped off, typical age rubs on generally well-preserved original finish. Comments: probably Dutch or Northern Germany, early-19th century. Value Points: compelling strong presence of the early doll, with well-defined carving of hair, artistic details of painting. $900/1300

135. Large American Wooden Dollhouse by Schoenhut with Lithographed Interior and Original Curtains

27" (69 cm.) x 23" x 23". The wooden two-story dollhouse has dimensional scored finish to simulate stone foundation and stone brick siding, The window and door frames are of sturdy pressed card stock with original cream finish; the front door is dark wood with natural finish, and the porch columns and balusters as well as wide front steps are of wood. The porch roof, which extends across the entire front is pressed card stock to simulate shingles and matching the upper roof shingles. There are eight interior rooms, a fancy wooden staircase to the second floor, and the walls are covered with lithographed wall paper and decorations that vary from room to room. Thirteen double pane windows have the original lace curtains, as does the front door window and the tiny gable window. The original Schoenhut label is on the side. Excellent condition, all original finishes, some small bends at roof corners. A very rare luxury size with rare to find interior finishes and curtains. Schoenhut, circa 1915. $1200/1800

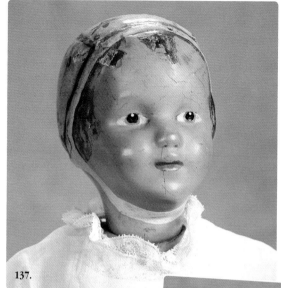

137.

137. American Wooden Girl with Sculpted and Painted Bonnet, Model 106, by Schoenhut

14" (36 cm.) All-carved wood, with socket head, carved hair in short bobbed fashion tucked beneath a carved Dutch style bonnet with cream-painted finish decorated with painted ribbons and flowers, painted blue eyes, accented nostrils, closed mouth with slightly-smiling expression, all-wooden spring-jointed body. Condition: very good, with some rubs and scuffing at edge of hair, body scuffed. Marks: Schoenhut Doll Pat. Jan.17,'11 USA & Foreign Countries (impressed). Comments: Schoenhut, the model was made for four years only, 1912-1916. Value Points: very rare model to find, with original finish, albeit with typical age wear, costume may be original, shoes and doll stand are original. $800/1200

138. American Carved Wooden Boy, Model 205, by Schoenhut

16" (41 cm.) All-carved wood, with socket head, deeply carved hair in short bobbed boyish fashion with overlapping curls at forehead, intaglio carved upper glancing blue eyes with pronounced black pupils in well-defined sockets,

136.

136. American Carved Wooden Twin Dolls, Model 105, by Schoenhut with Bobbed Hair and Hair Bands

14" (36 cm.) Each is all-carved wood, with socket head, carved hair in short bobbed fashion, carved head band with ribbon bow at the back, intaglio carved blue eyes in well-defined sockets, painted brows, accented nostrils, closed mouth with full pouting lips, all-wooden spring-jointed body. Condition: good, with some rubs and scuffing, blue band girl has old touch-up on nose. Marks: Schoenhut Doll Pat. Jan.17,'11 USA & Foreign Countries (impressed). Comments: Schoenhut, models 105, circa 1912. Value Points: the pair of twin dolls have superior sculpting indicative of early models, wearing antique matching dresses, one with pink hair band and having original Schoenhut shoes and stand, and the other with blue hair band. $800/1100

painted brows, accented nostrils, closed mouth with wide lips, all-wooden spring-jointed body. Condition: structurally good, many rubs and scuffing on head and body, unrestored. Marks: Schoenhut Doll Pat. Jan.17,'11 USA & Foreign Countries (impressed). Comments: Schoenhut, model 205, circa 1912. Value Points: very fine detail of carving on hair and features of the rare model. $500/700

139. American Carved Wooden Doll, Model 202, by Schoenhut

15" (38 cm.) All-carved wood, with socket head depicting an older boy or man, carved short hair with defined forelock curls, intaglio carved blue eyes in deeply set eye sockets, painted brows, accented nostrils, closed mouth with firmly-set lips, all-wooden spring-jointed body. Condition: some craquelure on nose and forehead, arms worn, unrestored Marks: Schoenhut Doll Pat. Jan.17,'11 USA & Foreign Countries (impressed). Comments: Schoenhut, model 202, the early model was made for a few years only, circa 1911. Value Points: very rare model with compelling expression, well-detailed carving especially of eyes. $500/800

140. American Carved Wooden Character Boy, Model 201, by Schoenhut

16" (41 cm.) All-carved wood, socket head with very full cheeks, carved short hair in tousled fashion with defined forelock curls, intaglio deeply-carved blue eyes, painted brows, accented nostrils, closed mouth with downcast pouting lips, all-wooden spring-jointed body. Condition: original finish is worn and scuffed. Marks: Schoenhut Doll Pat. Jan.17,'11 USA & Foreign Countries (impressed). Comments: Schoenhut, model 201, the early model was made for a few years only, circa 1911. Value Points: very rare model with well-detailed carving especially of crinkles around the eyes

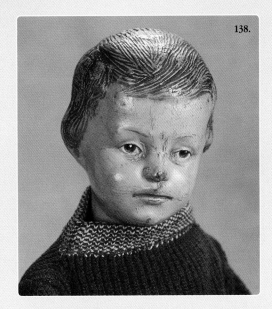

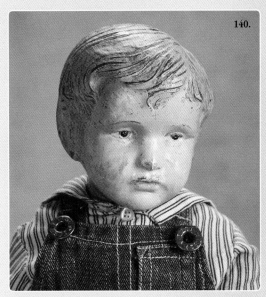

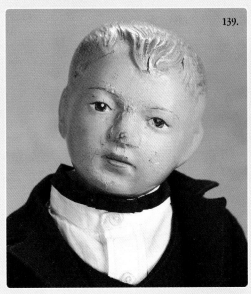

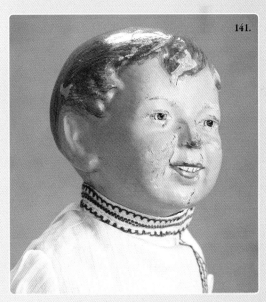

and mouth antique costume includes original Schoenhut shoes. $700/900

141. American Carved Wooden Boy, Model 203, by Schoenhut

16" (41 cm.) All-carved wood, socket head depicting a highly-characterized laughing boy, full cheeks, carved short hair in tousled fashion with defined forelock curls, intaglio deeply-carved blue eyes. painted brows, accented nostrils, closed mouth with beaming smile, painted row of teeth, all-wooden spring-jointed body. Condition: original finish is flaked and scuffed, hands worn. Marks: Schoenhut Doll Pat. Jan.17,'11 USA & Foreign Countries (impressed). Comments: Schoenhut, model 201, an early Graziano model, the doll was made for a few years only, circa 1911. Value Points: outstanding sculpting of facial features and hair, with realistic facial expression. $700/900

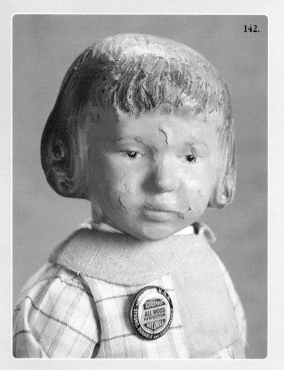

142.

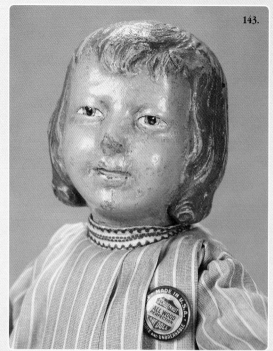

143.

144. Two American Wooden Dolls with Carved Braids, Models 102 and 103, by Schoenhut

14" (36 cm.) Each is all-wooden with carved socket head, carved hair with coiled braids, intaglio-carved eyes, painted features, all-wooden spring-jointed body, nicely costumed. Condition: with original finishes albeit quite rubbed and worn, the paint at back of hair on larger girl is worn away. Marks: Schoenhut Doll, Pat. Jan.17,'11 USA & Foreign Countries. Comments: Schoenhut, the larger doll is model 103 has large blue eyes with pronounced black pupils, detailed sculpting of hair around the forehead forming into narrow braids at the back; the smaller doll is model 102 and has small brown eyes with thickly-woven braids held by a pink bow at the back of her head, with original Schoenhut shoes. Value Points: two rare models depict variations on a common style. $700/1100

142. Rare American Wooden Girl, Model 100, with Sculpted Hair by Schoenhut

16" (41 cm.) All-carved wood with socket head, very full cheeks, sculpted hair with bangs and short bobbed curls, small intaglio painted downcast blue eyes, closed mouth with pouting expression, spring-jointed body, antique costume. Condition: scuffed and worn with some old retouch. Marks: Schoenhut Doll Pat. Jan 17, '11 USA & Foreign Countries. Comments: Schoenhut, model 100, from the Graziano years, the model was made for two years only. Value Points: very rare early model with well-rendered wistful expression, deeply-defined combmarks in unusual hair style. $600/900

143. American Wooden Smiling Girl, Model 103, with Sculpted Hair by Schoenhut

16" (41 cm.) All-wooden carved doll with socket head, sculpted hair in long ringlet curls with forelock curl onto forehead, deeply-set intaglio blue upper glancing eyes, tinged brows, accented nostrils, closed mouth with gentle smile, all-wooden spring-jointed body, nicely costumed. Condition: structurally excellent, extensive rubs on head and body. Marks: Schoenhut Doll Pat. Jan.17.'11 USA & Foreign Countries. Comments: Schoenhut, 1911, the rare model was made for less than one year. Value Points: extremely rare model with great attention to sculpting details especially of eyes and hair curls. $800/1000

144.

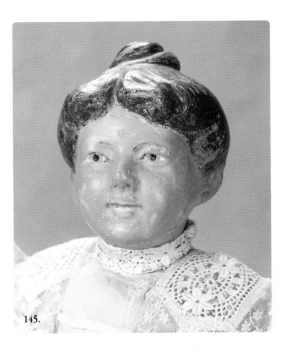

145.

145. American Carved Wooden Doll with Sculpted Topknot, Model 102, by Schoenhut

16" (41 cm.) Carved wooden socket head depicting an older girl or woman, with sculpted thick brown hair forming into curls around her forehead and captured into a topknot at the crown, intaglio blue eyes in deeply-set sockets, closed mouth, defined ears, all-wooden spring-jointed body, nicely costumed. Condition: structurally excellent, original painted finish is rubbed and worn. Marks: Schoenhut Doll Pat. Jan.17, '11 USA & Foreign Countries. Comments: Schoenhut, model 102, circa 1911, the model was created during the Graziano era. Value Points: very rare Schoenhut model with fine quality of sculpting. $700/900

146. American Wooden Smiling Girl, Model 101, with Bobbed Hair by Schoenhut

14" (36 cm.) All-carved wood with socket head, sculpted short curly bobbed hair waved away from her forehead and held by carved ribbon, painted brown eyes, closed mouth in impish smile with painted row of teeth, all-wooden spring-jointed body, costume may be original. Condition: very good overall. Marks: Schoenhut Doll Pat. Jan.17, '11 USA (decal mark). Comments: Schoenhut circa 1917. Value Points: pleasing cheerful expression and rare hair style on the smiling girl. $500/700

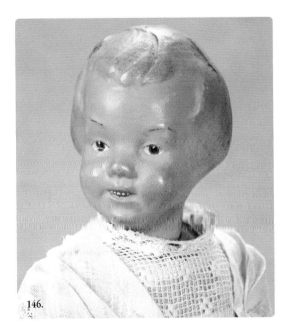

146.

147.

147. American Wooden Character by Schoenhut with Smiling Expression

10" (41 cm.) All-carved wood with socket head, intaglio deeply set blue eyes with pronounced black pupils, accented eye corners and nostrils, closed mouth with cheerful smile, row of painted teeth, blonde mohair bobbed wig over original frail wig, wooden spring-jointed body, wearing antique costume of striped cotton, straw hat. Condition: very good, some paint rubs and wear on nose and chin, body. Comments: Schoenhut, circa 1912. Value Points: rare model with pleasing expression, included is a small-wooden Schoenhut piano $700/900

patented by the artist in 1873, it is likely that they were made for some years prior to that. Included is a model with ringlet curls, especially detailed stitch-sculpting of ears, brown downcast eyes, and a model with short brown feathered curls and large brown eyes. Value Points: the rare and sought-after American doll is particularly charming as this pair with variant hair styles, posed on wooden bench with antique quilt. $9000/13,000

149. American Cloth Doll with Oil-Painted Features

15" (38 cm.) All-cloth doll with ball-shaped flat-dimensional head, having painted shaded brown curly hair, painted large brown eyes with black and red upper eyeliner, accented nostrils, closed mouth, blushed cheeks, muslin torso, sateen arms and legs, early cotton dress, undergarments, leather shoes. Condition: very good, original finish. Comments: American, circa 1890. Value Points: an appealing petite size, artistic painting of features. $700/900

148. Two Rare Early American Cloth Dolls by Izannah Walker

21" (53 cm.) Each is all-cloth with stiffened, pressed and oil-painted facial features and hair, depicting a young girl, having cotton sateen stitch-jointed body, oil-painted hands with stitched fingers, wearing early cotton dresses. Condition: good, finish is well worn. Comments: Izannah Walker of Rhode Island, mid-19th century, although the dolls were

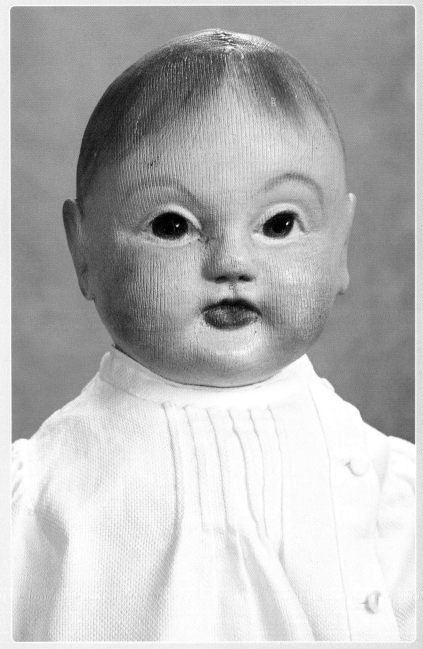

150. Rare American Brown-eyed Cloth Doll Known as Sheppard Baby

21" (53 cm.) All-cloth doll with firm-pressed stockinette head, painted brown hair with delicate feathering around the forehead, large brown eyes in defined eye sockets, arched brows, accented nostrils, closed mouth, very full cheeks, blushed ears, stockinette stitch-jointed body with oil painted lower arms and legs, separate thumbs, wearing white pique romper with leather ankle boots. Condition: generally excellent. Comments: American, circa 1880, the doll is known as Sheppard or Philadelphia Baby, in reference to its origin from the J. B. Sheppard department store of Philadelphia. Value Points: pristine condition of the rare American doll with realistic press-sculpting and most artistic painting of features. $1200/1800

153.

151. Rare American Black Stockinette Cloth Doll Attributed to Julia Beecher

19" (48 cm.) Firmly-stuffed black stockinette head with stitch-shaped facial features, cut-out eye sockets with eye whites, having painted lashes and black shoe-button eyes, embroidered brows, nostrils, red lips, black yarn hair cap, attached to original brown muslin body with stitch-jointing. Condition: very good, some old stitch repairs on face, hair worn away. Comments: attributed to Julia Beecher, of Elmira, New York, circa 1890, sister-in-law of Harriet Beecher Stowe. Value Points: rarely found doll with dear expression, sturdy body, original embroidery, fine old costume. $900/1300

152. Rare Early American Toy "The Myriopticon, A Historical Panorama" by Milton Bradley

8" (20 cm.) The boxed set is contained in its original box comprising a stage-like box with theatre curtains and on-looking people, that centers a long paper roll that depicts the historical panorama "Rebellion" according to the box title. The box is labeled Milton Bradley. Good condition, the roll is intact, although turning rods are missing, box cover worn. American, circa 1880. $400/600

153. American Papier-Mâché Doll "Miss Betty Barnard" by Ludwig Greiner

12" (30 cm.) Papier-mâché shoulder head with black sculpted hair arranged in rolls and curls, painted complexion and facial features, large blue eyes, single stroke brows, accented nostrils, closed mouth, muslin stitch-jointed body, leather sewn-on boots, nice antique dress and undergarments. Condition: generally excellent. Marks: Greiner's Patent Doll Heads No. 1 Pat. March 30, '58, Ext '72. Comments: Ludwig Greiner, Philadelphia, circa 1875. Value Points: rare size, fine original condition, the doll carries a little red calling card case with calling cards for "Miss Betty Barnard". $600/900

154. American Cast Iron Baby Cradle Attributed to J.& E. Stevens

7" (18 cm.) Fancily-scrolled open-work cast iron baby cradle with hood has original red and green finish. Very good original condition with some paint wear. Attributed to J. & E. Stevens, circa 1890. $300/500

155. American Early Raggedy Ann by Volland with 1915 Patent Date

16" (41 cm.) All-cloth doll with flat-dimensional face, rounded black shoe-button eyes on painted eye whites, short angled brows, six lashes under each eye, black-outlined red nose, thin line mouth with gentle smile, brown worsted wool hair, stitch-jointed body with heart on torso, red and white striped sewn-on stockings with brown sewn-on shoes. Condition: generally excellent. Marks: Patented Sept 7,1915. Comments: Raggedy Ann by Volland, early 1920s model, from designs by Johnny Gruelle. Value Points: well-preserved condition of the early model, wearing her original paisley print dress in shades of brown, cream, purple and green, with white pinafore and bloomers. $700/1100

156. 19th Century Rare American Toy by William Goodwin

11" (28 cm.) A papier-mâché shoulder head doll with black sculpted hair and painted facial features has wooden block torso, metal hands with curled fingers designed to hold the carriage handle bar, metal legs with disc-jointing at hips, and metal feet, is attached to a tin and cast iron three wheeled carriage, which, when wound, causes the girl to lift her feet up and down, thus moving the carriage along. Condition: very good, with some finish wear to cart, some craquelure on shoulder plate. Comments: American, William Goodwin, the keywind version of his patented walking lady, circa 1875. Value Points: rare early patented American toy. $600/800

157. American Patented Mechanical Doll by Goodwin

11" (28 cm.) A lady doll with pressed-cloth head in the manner of papier-mâché dolls has blonde sculpted hair with head band, painted earrings, painted facial features, original body with hidden mechanism, cast iron hands and feet, and is pushing a three-wheeled wooden cart with cast iron spoke wheels. The mechanism is wound by turning the left wheel clockwise, causing the doll to walk, thus pushing the carriage. Condition: very good/ excellent. Marks: W.H.F. Goodwin patents dated Jan 22, 1878 & August 25, 1868 (and) XLCR Doll Head Pat. Sept 8,1868 (labels on shoulders). Comments: the earliest version of the American toy patented by William Goodwin, with use of American doll head patented by George Hawkins. Value Points: rare American early toy is well preserved with original finish and costume. $800/1100

158. Rare Set of French Gilt Bronze Miniature Salon Furnishings

4"h. Of heavy cast bronze with exceptional detail of sculpting and accents, the salon furnishings are finished with a rich gold leaf; comprising a settee, six matching chairs and a table. Excellent condition. French, circa 1875, the luxury quality suggests the pieces were sold in a prestige Parisian store such as Maison Giroux. $500/800

159. Two German Bisque Miniature Dolls

6" (15 cm.) -7" dolls. Each doll has bisque shoulder plate with very pale complexion, blonde sculpted hair, blue glass inset eyes, painted lashes and brows, closed mouth, muslin body, bisque lower limbs, painted ankle boots, and is wearing a fine antique costume. Condition: generally excellent. Comments: Germany, circa 1880. Value Points: exquisite painting detail on the rare tiny size of the glass-eyed ladies. $500/700

160. Early French Bisque Poupée with Bisque Hands, Extensive Trousseau and Trunk

15" (38 cm.) Pale bisque shoulder head with plump face, cobalt blue glass eyes, dark eyeliner, painted lashes, feathered brows, accented nostrils, closed mouth with accent center line, brunette human hair hand-tied wig over cork pate, firmly-stuffed kid body with bisque arms to

160 accessories.

above the elbows, curled fingers. Condition: generally excellent. Comments: attributed to Blampoix, circa 1860. Value Points: included with the beautiful poupée is a wooden-domed trunk with various undergarments including hoop skirt, accessories including gloves, red leather Papeterie, box of bone dominoes, wooden snow shoes, and eight additional gowns of various styles $3500/4500

161. French Maple Wood Doll-Size Tall Chest with Marble Top

13" (33 cm.) Of maple wood with carved frame details to simulate bamboo, the tall chest features four drawers with wooden knobs and white marble top. Excellent condition. French, circa 1890. $300/500

163. Charming Petite French Bisque Bébé by Bru, Size 2, with Signed Bru Shoes

10" (25 cm.) Bisque socket head, large blue glass paperweight inset eyes, dark eyeliner, lushly-painted lashes, fringed brows, accented nostrils and eye corners, closed mouth with outlined lips, pierced ears, auburn mohair wig over cork pate, French composition and wooden fully-jointed body. Condition: generally excellent, original body and body finish. Marks: Bru Jne 2. Comments: Bru, circa 1890, the new style body was introduced by Girard at this time. Value Points: beautiful wide-eyed bébé with richly painted lips and brows, brilliant eyes, original body, and wearing original cotton dress, undergarments, socks, straw bonnet with silk band labeled "Le Mutin" in gilt, black silk parasol, and near-perfect original shoes signed "Bru Jne Paris 2". $7000/9500

164. Miniature German Bisque Doll with Toy Donkey

4 ½" (11 cm.) Bisque socket head, tiny glass eyes, painted features, closed mouth, brunette mohair wig, five-piece papier-mâché body. Condition: generally excellent. Marks: 4/0. Comments:

162. Wonderful French Bisque Bébé, Figure C, by Steiner in Antique Mariner Costume

10" (25 cm.) Bisque socket head, blue glass paperweight inset eyes, painted lashes, feathered brows, rose-blushed eye shadow, accented nostrils and eye corners, closed mouth, outlined lips with pronounced center line, pierced ears, blonde mohair wig over original Steiner pate, Steiner composition fully-jointed body. Condition: generally excellent, original body finish albeit rubbed. Marks" Figure C (n...0 partially illegible) Steiner Bte SGDG Paris. Comments: Jules Steiner, circa 1882. Value Points: rarer model to find in wonderful petite size, has choice bisque and painting, wonderful antique mariner costume, leather shoes, metal whistle. $3200/4500

Germany, circa 1890. Value Points: the little boy wears antique sailor costume including cap with gilt lettering "Douarnenez", along with a toy papier-mâché donkey with flannel cover, saddle, harness and glass eyes. $300/500

165. German All-Bisque Doll with Wooden Parlor Ensemble

4 ½" (11 cm.) doll. All-bisque doll with swivel head, blue glass eyes, painted features, closed mouth, pin-jointed limbs, painted stockings and blue two-strap shoes, blue cotton dress. Condition: generally excellent. Comments: Germany, circa 1900. Value Points: included is a 1900-era German wooden dollhouse parlor ensemble with three-column-pedestal round table, hanging mirror with shelves, dessert, cupboard with silver trim, and sofa with four matching chairs, each with original blue silk upholstery and fringe. $500/800

166. Five 19th Century Miniature Games

3" (8 cm.) nine-pin set box. Including set of wooden nine-pins in original box labeled "Hegelspiel, gesetz gesch"; carved bone dominoes in original slide-lid box; another set in glass-top box, roulette type game in original box; and Jeu de L'Oie in original slide lid box with instructions for play and original carved bone die and cups. Very good condition. French and Germany, late-19th century. $200/400

167. French Bisque Poupée with Wooden Articulated Lady Body

16" (41 cm.) Bisque swivel head on kid-edged bisque shoulder plate, blue glass enamel eyes, dark eyeliner, painted lashes, feathered brows, accented nostrils and eye corners, closed mouth with outlined lips, pierced ears, all-wooden body with dowel articulation at shoulders, elbows, wrists, hips, knees and ankles, and wooden ball pivot at waist, nicely costumed in grey serge walking suit, undergarments, silk bonnet and leather boots. Condition: generally excellent, tiny original firing mark at side lip, body is excellent but is not original. Marks: 4. Comments: Gaultier, circa 1875, with Bru deposed wooden poupée body. Value Points: lovely presence with fine bisque, and very rare body. $2800/3500

168. Beautiful Petite French Bisque Bébé by Gaultier, Early Block Letter Model

12" (30 cm.) Bisque swivel head on kid-edged bisque shoulder plate, blue glass paperweight inset eyes, dark eyeliner, painted dark lashes, feathered brows, accented nostrils and eye corners, closed mouth with pale accented lips, pierced ears, kid bébé body with square-cut collarette, gusset-jointed hips and knees, bisque lower arms. Condition: generally excellent, lower arms are antique albeit not original. Marks: F 5 G (block letters, head and shoulders). Comments: Gaultier, circa 1878, the earliest model of the Gaultier bébé with block letter marking and very rare original kid body. Value Points: compelling yet gentle presence, the little bébé wears fine antique aqua cashmere and velvet dress, undergarments, aqua kidskin shoes, and very delicate silk and lace bonnet. $2800/3800

169. Wonderful French Papier-Mâché Mechanical Walking Doll, Attributed to Theroude

10" (25 cm.) Solid domed papier-mâché head with black painted pate, tiny black enamel inset eyes, painted features, open mouth with two rows of teeth, shapely carton torso and legs, firm kid arms with stitched and separated finger, mounted upon a three-wheel tinplate base, wearing fine early costume of aqua silk with gilt paper appliques, lace hanky, silk flowers, undergarments, attached kidskin slippers, and velvet and silk trimmed bonnet over coiffe. When wound, the doll moves forward and to each side, turning her head, and moving her arms up and down as though enjoying the flowers she holds. Condition: generally excellent. Comments: French, circa 1850, attributed to Theroude. Value Points: an especially pleasing rare early doll with wonderfully-preserved costume, charming movements. $3500/5500

170. German All-Bisque Miniature Asian Doll, Probably Simon and Halbig

4 ½" (11 cm.) Amber-tinted solid domed bisque swivel head on bisque torso, brown glass inset eyes, painted angled brows, black painted lashes, closed mouth, peg-jointed bisque arms and legs, bare feet. Condition: generally excellent. Comments: attributed to Simon and Halbig, circa 1895. Value Points: rare to find model with all-original parts, original black mohair wig with long queue, and wearing original silk costume. $300/500

171. Collection of Accessories for French Poupées

3" (8 cm.) fan. Including carved bone folding fan with painted decorations, green wooden hat stand, green cardboard box containing original fur muff, green kidskin

gloves with wrist hooks, soft-metal chatelaine with various keys, miniature book with pressed gilt cover and velvet spine, bone hat stand, and very rare carved bone miniature book "Fabuliste du jeune age" with engravings. Excellent condition. French, mid-19th century. $400/700

172. German All-Bisque Brown-Complexioned Miniature Doll in Original Costume

4 ½" (11 cm.) Light-brown complexioned bisque swivel head on kid-edged bisque torso, peg-jointed bisque arms and legs, bare feet, brown glass enamel eyes, painted features, closed mouth, black mohair wig. Condition: generally excellent. Marks: 310.

Comments: Germany, circa 1890. Value Points: beautiful complexion on the rare doll, wearing her original silk costume with gilt paper accents, and gilt paper bracelets at ankles and wrists. $400/600

173. Tiny Rare German All-Bisque Asian Dolls with Sculpted Hair

2 ½" (6 cm.) Each is all-bisque with one-piece head and torso, peg-jointed arms and legs, amber-tinted complexion, black sculpted hair and painted facial features with brown eyes and side-slant brows, painted shoes. Condition: generally excellent. Comments: Germany, circa 1880. Value Points: the rare pair include man with black moustache and woman whose fancily-arranged hair is decorated with a yellow hair ornament, each with factory-original costume. $300/600

174. Rare German Wax Doll with Wire-Lever Eyes, Wooden Body and Original Costume

13" (33 cm.) Poured wax over papier-mâché shoulder head of lady doll with oval face and elongated throat, brown glass sleep eyes that operate from wire lever in torso, painted features, original brunette wig inserted into slit at crown and with coiled braid at the back, all-wooden body with shapely torso, articulation at shoulders, elbows, hips and knees, painted shoes, (frail) original muslin and lace gown. Condition: very good, some light craquelure, wire lever needs adjustment. Comments: Germany, circa 1840. Value Points: very rare early lady doll with original wig, wooden body, lever eyes, original costume. $600/900

6" (15 cm.) -7". Each has bisque shoulder head with sculpted hair and painted facial features, muslin body, bisque lower limbs, and is wearing factory-original costume. Condition: generally excellent. Comments: Germany, circa 1900. Value Points: each has rare feature, including man with very full beard and bushy moustache; young man with dark brown center-parted hair and elaborate sideburns; an identical model with light brown hair; older man with grey hair under silk top hat,

175. Six German Bisque Dollhouse Dolls in Service Outfits

6" (15 cm.) -7". Each has bisque shoulder head with sculpted hair, painted features, muslin body, bisque lower limbs, painted shoes, and each is wearing its factory-original costume to represent its position in the household. Condition: generally excellent. Comments: Germany, circa 1900. Value Points: included are chef with modeled sideburns, parlor maid with brown hair and high white stockings, chauffeur with moustache and oil-cloth uniform and boots; nanny with baby, kitchen helper with sculpted white cap, and housekeeper with chatelaine of keys. $800/1100

176. German Papier-Mâché Miniature Foods

3" (8 cm.) diam. plates. Each of the foods is presented on original cardboard plate with embossed borders; the food is realistically sculpted and painted, and includes roasts, fish, breads, torte, cucumbers, grapes, lobster, and more. Each plate is stamped Germany. Especially fine condition, and including rare food stuffs. Circa 1900. $500/800

and having very full unusual sideburns; black-complexioned man with glazed hair; and man with light brown hair and moustache. $900/1300

178. Amusing and All-Original French Mechanical Walking Doll

8" (20 cm.) Bisque socket head with blue glass eyes, painted features, closed mouth, pierced ears, blonde mohair wig, on carton torso containing mechanism, metal legs and feet. When wound, the doll slowly moves forward. Condition: generally excellent. Marks: 4/0. Comments: French, circa 1900. Value Points: the fashionable lady wears her original green flannel walking suit and bonnet with white flannel stole and muff. $500/800

179. German Bisque Boy with Sculpted Blonde Hair and Glass Eyes

13" (33 cm.) Bisque shoulder head with short blonde sculpted hair in side-parted fashion, blue glass enamel inset eyes, dark eyeliner, painted lashes and brows, accented nostrils and eye corners, closed mouth with center accent line, muslin stitch-jointed body with sewn-on stockings and blue kidskin shoes, antique gentleman's costume. Condition: generally excellent. Comments:

Germany, circa 1880. Value Points: very handsome model with beautiful bisque and painted features, rarer glass eyes. $400/600

180. All-Original German Papier-Mâché Doll with Walterhausen Bedroom Furnishings

8" (20 cm.) Papier-mâché shoulder head with blonde sculpted hair waved away from face in so-called "pumpkin" style, black enamel eyes, closed mouth, muslin body with carved wooden lower legs, painted black boots, wearing original gauzy gown, undergarments. Condition: very good, all original with typical rubs. Comments: Germany, circa 1875. Value Points: rare size with original costume, along with Walterhausen wooden furnishings with gilt-accented rosewood finish, including bed, sewing table with nice compartments, dresser with faux-ivory columns, metal clock under blown glass dome, bone opera glasses, porcelain dish, and woven carpet. $700/900

181. German Miniature "Medicine Chest for Dolls" for the English Market

3 ½" (9 cm.) The heavy card stock box designed as a hanging cupboard has a brass clasp, and gilt lettering "Medicine Chest for Doll". Inside are various bottles with stoppers, and the directory of ailments, viz. bronchitis, chicken-pox, chilbain, measles, sea-sickness, and whooping cough. Very rare doll accessory. Probably German for the English-Speaking market, circa 1890. $300/500

182. German Papier-Mâché Taufling Baby with High Chair and Rattle

9" (23 cm.) Solid domed papier-mâché head with dowel-attachment shoulder plate, black enamel eyes, painted features, closed mouth, muslin midriff with bellows crier, muslin upper legs, wooden legs and arms, papier-mâché hands and feet loosely-attached to simulate infant movements, antique baby gown and bonnet. Condition: generally excellent, original finish with some feature fading. Comments: Germany, circa 1860 the taufling baby was inspired by the Japanese Ichimatsu baby introduced at the London International Exhibition of 1851, and this model bears a remarkable resemblance. The doll is considered the inspiration for the classic child doll or bébé that followed. Value Points: sought-after and most appealing doll with historical significance; the doll is presented in an antique highchair, and owns an antique bone-handled rattle. $800/1000

183. Two German Papier-Mâché Taufling Babies and Early Bed

6" (15 cm.) Each has solid-domed papier-mâché head on swivel shoulder head, black enamel eyes, painted features, muslin midriff with interior bellows crier, wooden limbs with loosely-jointed hands and feet, antique costume. Condition: very good/excellent, original finishes with faded details, criers not working. Comments: Germany, circa 1860. Value Points: the rare models are delightful in this small size, one holds a tiny baby rattle, and the pair are presented in an early Walterhausen wooden doll bed. $900/1300

184. German Brown-Complexioned Taufling Baby

9" (23 cm.) Rich dark brown complexion swivel head on matching shoulder plate, sculpted black curly short hair, black enamel inset eyes, closed mouth with very full lips, brown muslin upper arms, upper legs and midriff, brown papier-mâché lower arms and legs, bare feet. Condition: generally excellent. Comments: Germany, circa 1860. Value Points: very rare and wonderfully-preserved doll with expressive features, fine original finish and body. $700/1100

185. Wonderful Collection of Early Miniature Dolls in Dome

3" (8 cm.) -5". Arranged on tiers under a glass dome are fourteen miniature dolls with sculpted hair, of bisque or porcelain, with muslin bodies, bisque or porcelain lower limbs, and wearing antique costumes. Condition: generally excellent. Comments: Germany, mid-19th century. Value Points: the wonderful variety of hair styles, mediums, facial expressions that were created in these early miniature dolls is beautifully exhibited in this case collection; the brown-haired lady with sculpted bodice is especially splendid, as the pink-tinted porcelain children are captivating in their expressions. $1200/1600

186. German Papier-Mâché Doll with Sculpted Cap and Feather, with Toys

10" (25 cm.) Wax over papier-mâché shoulder head depicting a young lad, with sculpted grey hat decorated with large feather, black enamel eyes, painted features, muslin body, wooden lower limbs. Condition: good, some typical paint fading. Comments: Germany, circa 1865. Value Points: rare sculpted hat, original blue cotton costume, and including an Erzebirge wooden toy cannon and five soldiers. $400/600

187. 19th-Century American Oil Painting "Child with Boy Doll in Red Hat"

19" (48 cm.) x 15" framed. The oil painting on canvas depicting a young child with softly-curled brown hair, wearing a white smock with detailed ruffles, along with a coral bead bracelet on each arm. The child is shown waist-up, a blue blanket covering its body, and clasping a beloved doll in both arms. The doll depicts a young boy which is a very rare feature in these painting, and is wearing an unusually-detailed costume with blue jacket, shirt, tie, embroidered trousers, shoes with defined laces, and a red cap with feather atop its head. Excellent condition. American, folk artist, mid-19th century. $2000/3500

188. Three German Papier-mâché Dolls with Wooden Articulated Bodies

5" (13 cm.) Each has papier-mâché head on shapely articulated wooden body with jointing at shoulders, elbows, hip and knees, sculpted hair in various styles, painted facial features, and each is wearing its original (frail) costume. Condition: very good/excellent, some dustiness. Comments: Germany, circa 1850. Value Points: very rare dolls made even more appealing with different facial expressions, rare wooden bodies. $700/1200

189. A Family of Tiny Grodnertal Wooden Dolls

3" (8 cm.) -3". Each is all-wooden with enamel painted complexion and lower limbs, painted hair with intricate details of curls, the man with painted goatee and the woman with sculpted tuck comb, painted facial features, all-wooden articulated body, painted shoes. Condition: generally excellent. Comments: Grodnertal, circa 1840, Value Points: rare to find these tiny wooden dolls in such fine state of preservation of painting, each wearing its original costume, and including woman with little wooden baby, and two men; also settee. $500/700

190. Two Miniature Grodnertal Wooden Dolls

2.2" (6 cm.) Each is all-wooden with one piece head and shapely torso, painted black hair with details of curls and one with sculpted tuck comb, painted facial features, dowel-jointing at shoulders, elbows, hips and knees, painted shoes, (frail) original costumes. Condition: generally excellent. Comments: Grodnertal, circa 1840. Value Points: wonderful state of preservation of the early dolls. $300/500

191. Fine English Wooden Two-Story Furnished Dollhouse
31" (79 cm.) l. x 27"h. x 17"d. The wooden two-story doll house has original painted finish to appear as though stone, with double chimneys that extend the full height of the house, framed wooden windows and doors with elaborate detail, the two first floor windows being three-sided and the front door with deeply paneled design. The four room interior has original (extremely worn) wall papers, wooden floors, and is wonderfully furnished with antique furnishings, accessories, chandeliers, lamps, pets, dishes and glassware, one room designed as a music room with appropriate accessories, and 12 antique bisque dolls of the 1880 era. Original exterior finish is well-preserved. English, mid-19th century. $4000/6000

193. 18th-Century Poured Wax Miniature Bristle Doll and Bone Piano

3 ½" (9 cm.) Poured wax shoulderhead of adult lady, faded painted facial features, wooden torso, wax arms, "bristle" legs. Condition: fair/good, lacking wig. Comments: the doll is shown in Ackerman's *Dolls in Miniature*, page 54, described as of the 18th century and noting her "graceful and feminine qualities" most notable for her tiny size. Value Points: the very rare doll wears her frail original

costume, and is presented in a glass dome along with an early carved bone piano (some few flakes at crest trim) with rare bone music sheet and candle sticks. $400/600

194. German Porcelain Gentleman with Rare Wooden Articulated Body

8" (20 cm.) Porcelain shoulder head with sculpted short black hair, defined curls around the

192. 18th-Century Leather Gentleman with Original Elaborate Silk Costume

7" (18 cm.) The very slender and elongated gentleman has a firmly-shaped leather head with embroidered features including teeth, prominent nose, stitched-on thread wig with lengthy plait at the back, wrapped armature body. Condition: fair/good, overall dustiness. Comments: 18th century, the doll is shown in Ackerman's *Dolls in Miniature*, page 46, described as a "fashionably dressed man" likely made for presentation in early baby houses. Value Points: he is wearing his original silk costume with brown silk coat and fitted breeches, embroidered vest, and is displayed under a glass dome with a miniature Walterhausen wooden desk. $600/900

face, painted facial features, wooden slender torso and upper limbs, porcelain lower limbs, dowel-jointing at shoulders, elbows, hips and knees, painted orange shoes, antique costume. Condition: generally excellent, repair to one porcelain knee dowel. Comments: Germany, circa 1850. Value Points: rare early porcelain with sought-after body style. $700/900

195. Set of German Walterhausen Dollhouse Furnishings in Original Box

6" (15 cm.) h. armoire. The bentwood lidded box contains an original assortment of wooden dollhouse furnishings decorated with ebony papers accented with gilt garlands and designs, including armoire, sofa with green velvet upholstery, secretary desk, chest of drawers, toilette, night stand, upright piano, and six chairs with green silk upholstery. Very good condition, original finishes, piano is missing keyboard lid. Germany, Walterhausen, attributed to D.H. Wagner & Sohne, circa 1885. $700/1100

196. A Family of Early Grodnertal Miniature Wooden Dolls

4" (10 cm.) largest. Each is all-carved wood with one-piece head, elongated throat, and shapely torso, dowel-jointing at shoulders, elbows, hips and knees and each has painted complexion and black hair with dainty curls around her face, (and four with sculpted yellow tuck combs), painted facial features and blush, antique costumes. Condition: very good, original finishes, some costume fraility, one tuck comb and one leg missing. Comments: Grodnertal, circa 1840. Value Points: a wonderful family group of rare early dolls, each with different

expressive features and hair paint are posed seated on early miniature sofa. $900/1300

197. Set of Miniature Dishes

1" (3 cm.) Possibly of carved agate, the tiny set has painted decorations to enhance the natural marbled finish, and includes plates, bowls, goblets, vases, and other pieces. Excellent condition. $200/300

198. French Early Bent-Wire Garden Furnishings with Porcelain Dolls

6 ½" (17 cm.) dolls. The intricately bent and shaped wire furnishings include a serving table with shelves, oval table, six side chairs and a long sofa with arched back. Along with two porcelain dolls with black sculpted hair, depicting a man and woman, each with painted facial features, muslin body, porcelain lower limbs, and each wearing its original costume. Condition: generally excellent. Comments: the furniture is French, mid-19th century; dolls are German, circa 1875. Value Points: very rare furniture in beautifully-preserved condition, enhanced by doll companions and their miniature porcelain tea service. $800/1300

199. French Early Bent-wire Furnishings with a Family of Porcelain Dolls

6 ½" (17 cm.) mother. The early bent wire furnishings includes a swinging cradle, bed, and three drawer chest. Along with a porcelain shoulder head lady with sculpted short hair, muslin body, porcelain limbs, antique costume, and three all-porcelain babies in the so-called "Frozen Charlotte" pose, one with very fine pink-tinted complexion, and another with sculpted smock. Condition:

generally excellent. Comments: furniture is French, mid-19th century, dolls are Germany, circa 1875. Value Points: very rare to find furnishings with beautiful details of bent and scrolled designs. $700/1200

200. German Pressed Tin Gazebo, Probably Maerklin, with Window Boxes, and Four Dollhouse People

12" (30 cm.) w. x 14"h. The pressed tin outdoor gazebo with pierced lattice design and fleur-de-lis edging has four corner columns, roof, painted green floor to simulate tile, and three attached painted tin window boxes with gilt edging and wooden flower pots. Included are four bisque dollhouse dolls, each with sculpted hair, muslin bodies and bisque lower limbs, the women with inset glass eyes and the men with moustaches. Excellent condition overall. Germany, circa 1900, a rare outdoor tin room. $800/1300

201. Seventeen French All-Bisque Miniature Dolls in Original Costumes

2 ½" (6 cm.) Each is all-bisque with swivel head, peg-jointed bisque arms and legs, bare feet or painted shoes, painted facial features, mohair wig. Condition: generally excellent, some costume dustiness. Comments: French, circa 1900, the series was presented in Parisian Etrennes catalogs of the era. Value Points: delightful and beautifully designed miniatures dolls are wearing their factory original costumes. $800/1400

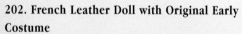

203.

202. French Leather Doll with Original Early Costume

10" (25 cm.) The firmly-stuffed all-brown-leather doll has shaped features including nose, chin and tiny mouth, defined neck, with cut-out eye sockets, applied pupils, painted brows, black wiry hair and is wearing her original costume of transfer printed cottons, wrapped turban and jewelry. Condition: generally excellent. Comments: for the French market, late-19th century, the doll was designed to represent women of the Martinique Islands. An article about the dolls appeared in the French journal *L'Illustration* at that time. Value Points: rare to find doll with excellent construction details and imaginative design, is well-preserved. $800/1200

203. Two German Bisque Miniature Dolls with Horse, Trunk and Little Toys

4 ½" (11 cm.) larger. Each has bisque socket head, five-piece papier-mâché body, closed mouth, one with painted eyes, the other with blue glass eyes, mohair wig and antique costume. Condition: generally excellent. Marks: 4/0 860 (larger). Comments: Germany, circa 1890. Value Points: included with the boys is a hide-covered papier-mâché horse with elaborate harness and amber glass eyes, a wooden trunk with lithographed paper cover to simulate wood and leather trim, and miniature toys including Erzebirge wooden dolls, swings and animals, and a wonderful little papier-mâché piglet. $800/1300

204.

204. German All-Bisque Miniature with Trunk, Christmas Tree, and Many Little Toys

5" (13 cm.) One-piece bisque head and torso, brown glass eyes, painted features, closed mouth, blonde mohair wig, peg-jointed bisque arms and legs, painted shoes and socks, and wearing wonderful factory-original costume. Condition: generally excellent. Marks: 67-4. Comments: Germany, circa 1900. Value Points: the all-original little boy is presented along with an antique miniature trunk containing a miniature feather tree with ornaments, golden mohair teddy, four tiny miniature dolls, tiny toy horse, soft-metal high chair, brass binoculars, birdcage, skates, and wooden ball and stick game. $800/1100

206. Rare French Brown-Complexioned Bisque "Paris Bébé" by Danel Et Cie

13" (33 cm.) Bisque socket head with cafe-au-lait light brown complexion, amber brown glass inset eyes, light brown brush-stroked brows, accented nostrils, closed mouth with accented lips, pierced ears, dark brown human hair over cork pate, French brown composition and wooden fully-jointed body, wearing lovely antique costume and bonnet, antique black leather boots with brown pom-poms, undergarments. Condition: generally excellent, tiny nose rub. Marks: Paris Bébé Depose 3 (incised). Comments: Danel & Cie of Paris, circa 1890; the doll model was the cause of a lawsuit between Jumeau and Danel, resulting in the Danel Paris Bébé being withdrawn from the market; made for one year only, few models exist, and the brown-complexioned model is extremely rare. Value Points: charming presence of the rare doll. $3500/5500

206, 207.

207. German Papier-mâché and Fur Pull Toy Goat

9" (23 cm.) The firm papier-mâché standing goat with wooden hooves, has fluffy white fur coat, glass eyes, leather ears, defined mouth, and is posed upon a wooden pull-toy base with cast iron wheels. Very good condition, some dustiness to fur. Germany, circa 1885, the luxury toy has original harness. $700/900

208. Collection of German Papier-mâché Novelty Candy Containers

3 ½" (9 cm.) football. Each is of papier-mâché or card stock with decorative lithographed finish, including pair of heeled dance shoes with crepe paper ruffles, football, champagne container with bottle, accordion, violin case, hat box with steamer labels, and world globe on wooden base. Each piece separates to reveal hollow interior for use as candy container. Excellent condition. Germany, circa 1900, a wonderful variety of charming bygone ephemera in beautifully-preserved condition. $500/800

208.

209. Collection of Palmer Cox Brownie Ephemera

8" (20 cm.) figurine. Including a softpaste Brownie candleholder, impressed 2602, two lithographed cloth Brownies, small softpaste mug, "Another Brownie Book" by Palmer Box (1890), Tintograph Brownie Stencils in original box, Brownie Stamps and Coloring Outfit in original box by Baumgarten & Co of Baltimore, and a "Brownies Ladder" wooden toy with lithographed paper designs. Candle holder, cloth dolls, and Brownie Stamps excellent, others played with in fair/good condition. Circa 1895. $500/800

210. German Bisque Miniature Doll in Original Costume, with Furnishings

5" (13 cm.) Bisque shoulder head with sculpted brown hair waved away from face and held by a black painted band, with finger curls at the back, painted facial features, muslin body, bisque lower limbs, black painted boots. Condition: generally excellent, left front foot chipped off. Comments: Germany, circa 1875. Value Points: rare early miniature doll with brown hair, wearing factory original military costume. Included is a set of wooden dollhouse furnishings with lithographed paper cover, possibly Bliss. $400/700

211. Two German Paper Dolls Known as Milliner's Models

8" (20 cm.) and 9". Each has papier-mâché shoulder head with sculpted black hair, painted facial features, slender kid body, wooden lower limbs, painted shoes. Condition: generally excellent, finish on man a bit dusty. Comments: Germany, circa 1840. Value Points: the woman has large turquoise eyes and elaborate coiffure with painted stippled curls around her face, and the man has well-detailed short curly hair, both wearing original costumes. $500/700

213. German Papier-mâché Doll by Greiner with Pull-Toy Horse

14" (36 cm.) Papier-mâché shoulder head with black sculpted hair curled behind her fully-sculpted ears, short finger curls, dark painted upper glancing eyes, painted

curly upper lashes, closed mouth, muslin stitch-jointed body, leather arms, wearing fine antique dress, undergarments, kidskin slippers. Condition: generally excellent, nose rub, body especially clean and sturdy. Marks: Greiner's Improved Patent heads Pat. March 30th '58. (paper label). Comments: Ludwig Greiner of Philadelphia, circa 1860. Value Points: desirable early patent date model in charming size, antique costume. Along with canvas-covered wooden horse on original wooden base with cast iron wheels and original saddle and harness. $800/1300

91 German Wooden Noah's Ark with Animals

12" (30 cm.) All-wooden Noah's Ark has original painted details of windows and vine-covered roof which hinges open to reveal an assortment of small-carved wooden animals. Ark is excellent, animal pairs are not complete. Germany, circa 1880. $300/500

215, 216.

215. Pretty French Bisque Brown-Eyed Bébé by Rabery and Delphieu

14" (36 cm.) Bisque socket head, amber brown glass paperweight inset eyes with spiral threading, long dark painted lashes, single stroke brows, closed mouth with center accent line, accent dots at nostrils and eye corners, pierced ears, brunette mohair wig over cork pate, French composition and wood fully-jointed body, pretty antique costume. Condition: generally excellent. Marks: R 3/0 D. Comments: Rabery and Delphieu, circa 1890. Value Points: pretty child with large brown eyes, original body and body finish. $1800/2500

216. French Wooden Toilette Table with Marble Top and Accessories

14" (36 cm.) The cherry-wood finished toilette table with shapely legs, center drawer, white marble top, and attached hinged mirror is fitted with a white porcelain washbowl and pitcher set accented with gilt borders. Excellent condition, mirror faded. French, circa 1880. $400/600

217. Eleven Tiny German All-Bisque Dolls in Original Knit Costumes

1 ½" (4 cm.) Each is all bisque with pin-jointed arms and legs, painted hair and facial features, painted shoes and stockings. Condition: generally excellent. Comments: Germany, circa 1890. Value Points: the set of tiny dolls are wearing factory-original knit costumes representing school children, Japanese girl, folklore costumes, and historical costumes. $300/500

218. Tiny French Bisque Bébé by Jules Steiner with Original Signed Body

8" (20 cm.) Bisque socket head, brown glass enamel inset eyes, painted lashes, feathered brows, accented nostrils and eye corners, closed mouth with accent line between the lips, pierced ears, lambswool wig over Steiner pate, French composition body with jointing at shoulders, elbows and hips, nice antique costume and bonnet, coral necklace and earrings. Condition: generally excellent. Marks: A 1 (head, incised) (Steiner stamp on torso). Comments: Jules Steiner, circa 1890. Value Points: most delightful and rare tiny size with pleasing bisque and painting, original signed body. $1100/1500

218, 219, 220.

219. An All-Original French Pull-Toy "Two Clowns at Play"

11" (28 cm.) A wooden base with spoked iron wheels is decorated with lithographed paper having unusual design of fans, candy cones and playing cards and is edged with gilt paper border. Atop the base are two bisque dolls, first, a young boy standing behind a decorated wooden drum, with drumsticks in his hands, and secondly, a young boy who is seated on a high wooden swing that suspends between two decorated poles. Each doll is dressed as a clown with well detailed ruffles and gilt paper trim, and has glass eyes, closed mouth, and mohair wig. When pulled along, playful movements occur. Condition: generally excellent, slight costume fading, tiny flake at one eye corner. Comments: for the French market, circa 1890. Value Points: well-preserved delightful toy with luxury details such as unusual paper design on base, and gilt paper trim. $1200/1800

220. French Papier-mâché Clown with Unusual Horse Decorations

14" (36 cm.) Papier-mâché socket head, blue glass inset eyes, painted facial features, open mouth, white lambswool wig, French papier-mâché body with jointing at shoulders and hips. Condition: generally excellent, costume a bit faded. Comments: French, circa 1900. Value Points: the clown, who is wearing his original silk jester costume with pom-pom trim, has unusual horse-themed clown decorations on his face, along with typical clown designs. $400/500

221, 222.

closed mouth with outlined lips, pierced ears, blonde mohair wig over cork pate, French composition and wooden fully-jointed body. Condition: generally excellent, body finish original albeit scuffed. Marks: F. G (in scroll) 1. Comments: Gaultier, circa 1885. Value Points: very dear bébé in charming size, lovely bisque and painting, original muslin chemise, bonnet, leather shoes. $1800/2300

223. Three German Bisque Miniature Dolls with Rare Furnishings

6" (15 cm.) largest. Each doll has bisque shoulder head with blonde sculpted hair, painted facial features, muslin body, bisque lower limbs, painted shoes. Condition: generally excellent, the larger has one broken foot. Comments: Germany, circa 1875, wonderful variations of hair styles on the small dolls, antique costumes, the larger with especially fine factory original gown. Value Points: included with the rare little dolls is a set of fine pinewood furniture with gilt paper beaded edging, including toilette table with canopy top, round front curio with lithograph scene, hall mirror, table, settee, and six chairs with original (frail) pink silk upholstery. $800/1200

224. Wonderful and Rare German Parade Pull Toy

21" (53 cm.) A papier-mâché dappled horse with flannel coat is posed as though prancing, with decorative harness and parade feathers and amber glass eyes, attached to a wheel base and pulling a fanciful woven wicker cornucopia sleigh that is decorated with lace and silk flowers. Seated in the sleigh is a bisque head girl with glass eyes, closed mouth, brunette mohair wig, wearing her original coral silk

221. Wonderful French Maple Wood Doll Furniture in Rare Petite Size

11" (28 cm.) h. buffet. Of maple wood with natural finish and having faux-bamboo edging, the set comprises a buffet with cupboard base and upper open shelves, unusual octagonal-shaped table with fancy pedestal base, and four matching chairs with original rose cotton print upholstery edged in pink braid. Excellent condition. French, circa 1880, very rare size in perfectly-preserved condition, wonderful for display with petite bébés or larger mignonettes. Miniature porcelain dishes are included. $700/900

222. Petite French Bisque Bébé, Size 1, by Gaultier in Original Chemise

9 ½" (24 cm.) Bisque socket head, brown glass enamel inset eyes, painted lashes, feathered brows, accented nostrils,

223.

225.

and lace gown and bonnet. The sleigh rests upon two large spoked wheels and two small tin wheels. When pulled along, the horse prances up and down. Condition: generally excellent, one small tin wheel lacking which does not affect the action. Comments: Germany, late-19th century. Value Points: wonderful and imaginative toy depicting a storyland parade float. $2000/3000

225. French All-Bisque Mignonette with Jointed Leg Dog

4 ½" (11 cm.) Solid domed bisque swivel head on kid-edged bisque torso, bright blue glass inset eyes, long painted lashes, single stroke brows, accented nostrils and eye corners, closed mouth with accent line between the full lips, peg-jointed bisque arms and legs, painted shoes, antique costume.

Condition: generally excellent.

Comments: French, circa 1888. Value Points: very expressive features with slight smile, large eyes, along with an all-bisque dog with painted neck bow and pin-jointed legs. $500/800

224.

size with very expressive gentle features, wearing original muslin print gown and undergarments, lace cap with silk flowers and black velvet streamers. $1200/1600

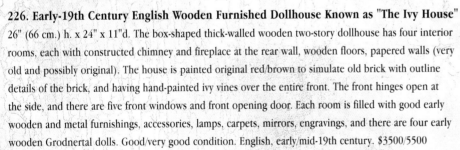

226. Early-19th Century English Wooden Furnished Dollhouse Known as "The Ivy House"
26" (66 cm.) h. x 24" x 11"d. The box-shaped thick-walled wooden two-story dollhouse has four interior rooms, each with constructed chimney and fireplace at the rear wall, wooden floors, papered walls (very old and possibly original). The house is painted original red/brown to simulate old brick with outline details of the brick, and having hand-painted ivy vines over the entire front. The front hinges open at the side, and there are five front windows and front opening door. Each room is filled with good early wooden and metal furnishings, accessories, lamps, carpets, mirrors, engravings, and there are four early wooden Grodnertal dolls. Good/very good condition. English, early/mid-19th century. $3500/5500

227. Diminutive English Carved Wooden Doll in Antique Gown
9" (23 cm.) Egg-shaped carved wooden head with elongated neck and shapely torso, flat back, cloth arms, crudely-shaped wooden legs with dowel-jointing at hips and knees, with narrow enamel inset eyes, painted dots as lashes and brows, closed mouth, brunette human hair. Condition: original finish well-preserved except nose rub. Comments: England, late 18th century. Value Points: rare diminutive

227.1. Early Nuremberg Wooden Kitchen with Extensive Copper and Pewter Ware

23" (58 cm.) x 19" x 14". The two-walled wooden kitchen with thick walls and floor has built-in wooden chimney, stove, shelving and counters with natural and dark green painted finish; the floor has square-defined outlines as though stone, and there is a wooden table and two chairs. The kitchen is furnished with a set of copper mugs supported by dowels on the shelf top, and there are numerous additional copper pots, kettles, and pudding molds ; unusual turned wooden coffee pot and dishes, pewter goblets and cups and saucers, pewter covered tureens, and tinware including lantern, double coffee maker with wooden handle, and many more utensils. Very good/excellent condition. Original finishes with typical age patina wear and rubs. Germany, Nuremberg, mid-19th century. $3000/4500

228. Set of Four Early Books "The Story of Miss Dollikins"

5" (13 cm.) x 3". The set of four books have pale rose hard covers with very stylized design, and contain wonderful stories of Miss Dollikins who "spent the first days of her life in the window of a large toy shop in London", as well as engravings that illustrate the stories. Published by T. Nelson and Sons, London, 1870. Good/very good condition. A charming and rare series. $200/400

229.

229. Rare Early-19th Century Dollhouse Furnishings including Rock and Graner

4" (10 cm.) h. buffet. Including tin buffet with lattice-work edging, and credenza with hinged lid and green gargoyle legs, each with original faux-rosewood painted finish. Along with a cast iron mangle (one small piece broken off of grip), wonderful wooden bellows with original cream painted finish, a bone-handled hammer with cast iron head, and a cast iron mantel clock with porcelain face having raised markings on the back "A.E. Hotchkiss Patent Nov.21,1876". Excellent condition. A rare group of dollhouse miniatures from the mid-1800s. $800/1300

230. Four Miniature Glass Bottles in Original Box

2 ½" (6 cm.) bottles. Four blown glass bottles are preserved inside an early box with engraving on its lid; the bottles each are labeled with a canceled 1 cent US stamp with semi-profile image. Excellent condition. The box is pencil dated Dec. 25, '71 on the inside lid. $100/200

230.

231. German Papier-mâché Doll with So-Called Bee-Hive Coiffure

11" (28 cm.) Papier-mâché shoulder head with heart-shaped face, sculpted black hair with deeply-impressed curls and so-called bee-hive arrangement at the crown, painted turquoise eyes, closed mouth, slender kid body, wooden lower limbs, wearing (frail) antique bronze green silk gown, undergarments. Condition: very good, original finish,

231.

minor paint wear on hair, one small craquelure at lower back. Comments: Germany, circa 1840. Value Points: rare coiffure, original finish and costume, painted yellow shoes. $500/700

232. Petite German Porcelain Doll and Wooden Cabinet

6 ½" (17 cm.) Porcelain shoulder head with black sculpted hair arranged with short finger curls, painted facial features, muslin body, pink-tinted porcelain lower arms, painted porcelain ankle boots, antique gown and undergarments. Condition: generally excellent. Comments: Germany, circa 1860. Value Points: especially nice modeling of features with excellent painting, original costume, included is a wooden dessert buffet with fancy architectural details and silver hardware. $300/500

232.

233, 234.

235.

236.

233. Four German Wooden Miniature Bristle Dolls

2" (5 cm.) Each is all-wooden with loosely-hinged legs that suspend between wire pins that are designed to allow the doll to "dance", each with original painted facial features, hair, and vibrant costume in variation of styles. Excellent condition, Germany, circa 1880. $300/500

234. Rare German Porcelain Doll with Wooden Body, and Early Bentwood Furnishings

9" (23 cm.) Porcelain shoulder head with light pink tinted complexion, black sculpted hair in short finger curls, painted blue eyes, red and black upper eyeliner, accented nostrils, shapely wooden torso and wooden upper limbs, porcelain lower limbs with attached porcelain dowels, dowel-jointing at shoulders, elbows, hips and knees, painted black ankle boots. Condition: generally excellent. Comments: Germany, circa 1850. Value Points: rare model is well-preserved, along with a set of black bentwood furnishings with original velvet and wool braid trim. $800/1200

235. German Porcelain Miniature Doll with Rare Wooden Body

5" (13 cm.) Porcelain shoulder head with black sculpted hair, pink tinted complexion, painted facial features, tiny blue eyes, shapely wooden torso and legs, dowel-jointing at shoulders and hips, porcelain lower limbs, painted shoes, wearing gentleman's woolen suit. Condition: generally excellent. Comments: Germany, circa 1850. Value Points: rare wooden body and finely painted features. $300/600

236. German Porcelain Miniature Doll with Wooden Body

5" (13 cm.) Porcelain shoulder head with black sculpted hair having shaped curls around the forehead, painted facial features, bright blue eyes, wooden torso and upper limbs, dowel-jointing at shoulders, elbows, hips and knees, painted shoes, wearing gentleman's woolen suit. Condition: generally excellent. Comments: Germany, circa 1860. Value Points: rare little doll with wooden body, antique costume. $300/400

237, 238.

237. Larger American Wooden Doll by Joel Ellis in Original Costume

15" (38 cm.) Carved wooden head with gesso and painted finish, having short black ringlet-curled hair, painted brown eyes, (faded) painted features and lips, shapely-wooden torso with dowel-jointed wooden arms and legs, metal hands and feet with painted ankle boots. Condition: good, original finish unrestored with paint wear and rubs on head and lower limbs. Comments: Joel Ellis, Vermont, circa 1885. Value Points: good large size in excellent structural condition, wearing original gown and undergarments. $700/900

238. Rare American Set of Wooden ABC Doll Furniture by Bliss

6" (15 cm.) l. sofa. Of pinewood with lithographed paper designs in rich in architectural details encircling alphabet letters, the ensemble comprises the complete alphabet except x and z. Including sofa, five side chairs, footstool, upright piano and stool, and a parlor game table with checkerboard design top. Excellent condition. American, probably Bliss, late-19th century. $400/500

239. Early American Book "Paper Dolls' Furniture" by Allair, 1857

8" (20 cm.) x 6". The soft bound book with embossed leather-like cover has gilt lettering "Paper Dolls Furniture" on the cover. The title page includes the sub-

title "How to Make it", by C.B. Allair, published by Anson D.F. Randolph, New York 1857, and contains 63 pages with illustrations and directions on constructing furniture for paper dolls. The book is complete albeit with rough edges, some spotting. A rare find. $200/400

240. Two German Bisque Miniature Dolls and Early Furnishings

7 ½" (19 cm.) Each has bisque shoulder head with blonde sculpted hair, painted facial features, bisque lower limbs, painted shoes, including lady with long ringlet curls and wearing antique lace gown (hairline front shoulder plate), and boy with short cropped painted hair, wearing original Tyrolean costume with green velvet vest, black breeches, and red leather suspenders. Condition: excellent except as noted. Comments: Germany, circa 1870. Value Points: rare early models with unusually expressive features for such tiny dolls, original costume on boy is especially fine. Included is a set of wooden doll furniture, possibly Bliss, with colorful lithographed paper cover to simulate carving and upholstery. $700/900

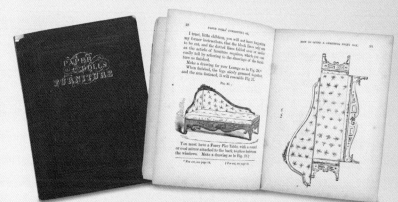

239.

240.

241.

241. Early American Boxed Game "Panorama of the Visit of Santa Claus"

8" (20 cm.) x 5 ½". A firm-sided box with marbled finish lid that is decorated with engravings of children at play (including a little girl with doll) has title "Panorama of The Visit of Santa Claus to the Happy Children", by Milton Bradley of Springfield, Mass. Inside is a stage-like construction that features a rolled scroll of engravings of children at play. An original advertisement is included which details the exhibition of art that originally accompanied the game presentation. Fair condition of box and roll mechanism, scroll engravings are very good with fresh colors. A very rare presentation, penciled on the interior lid "Walter A. Fisher, A Christmas gift from his mother". From the earliest period of the legendary game company, circa 1860s. $200/400

242. American Folk Art Carved Wooden Gentleman

22" (56 cm.) Carved wooden shoulder head of slender adult man with sculpted brown side-parted hair with very full side burns in front of sculpted ears, sculpted features, blue upper glancing painted eyes, accented nostrils, closed mouth with outlined lips, muslin firmly-stuffed body, wooden lower limbs, painted shoes,

242.

of that antique gentleman's formal wear ensemble. Condition generally excellent, some paint wear on shoulder plate. Comments: American, late-19th century. Value Points: the ingenious artfulness of the folk artist contrasts with refined presentation of the society gentleman. $800/1100

243. Seven German Bisque Dollhouse Dolls in Service

5" (13 cm.) -6". Each has bisque shoulder head with sculpted hair and painted facial features, muslin body, bisque lower limbs, painted shoes, and factory original costume. Condition: generally excellent. Comments: Germany, circa 1900. Value Points: rare models include black-complexioned butler, cook with bisque cap, chauffeur with bisque cap, parlor maid with sculpted white hair band, and three additional servants. $800/1200

244. Five German Bisque Dollhouse Dolls

6" (15 cm.) Each has bisque shoulder head with sculpted hair, painted facial features, muslin body, bisque lower limbs, original or antique costume. Condition: generally excellent. Comments: Germany, circa 1910. Value Points: included are Grandpa with grey hair and strong jaw line, Grandma with grey hair and chignon, brown-haired man with long sideburns, woman with elaborately

arranged hair, and young woman (school teacher?) with brown hair in bun and having painted spectacles. $500/900

245. The 19th Century English Arnold J. Wilson Wooden Dollhouse and Furnishings

27" (69 cm.) h. x 20" x 18". The thick-walled wooden two-story dollhouse has walnut framed windows and door, and paneled front double doors; there are four windows on each side. The front hinges open above three step stairs and basement crawl space with window cut outs. Two rooms are on each floor with arched door openings between, and the house is well-furnished with antique period furnishings, chandeliers, lamps, carpets and accessories. There are four porcelain dollhouse dolls in antique costumes within. Very good condition, wall paper is retained on one wall, other walls and floor are natural unfinished wood. There is a brass name plate "Arnold J. Wilson" at the front. Mid-19th century, probably English. $3000/4500

246. German Musical Vignette "Mary and Her Little Lamb"

9" (23 cm.) overall h. 9"l. Standing upon a wooden base with hidden musical bellows that plays a tune when squeezed and released, is a bisque head doll with brown glass eyes, painted features, closed mouth, blonde mohair wig, wood block torso, papier-mâché limbs, wearing original costume, alongside her little fleecy lamb with velvet blanket and leather harness. Excellent condition. Germany, circa 1890. A charming musical vignette. $800/1100

247. Three Early Puzzles in Original Boxes

Including early wooden jigsaw puzzle with engraved images, in original wooden tiny box with slide lid (one piece missing); set of six six-sided blocks with different engraved images on each side, in original slide lid box, and with pages of three of the images that could be created; and rare early puzzle game of Milton Bradley "Dissected Pictures" in original box, with picture images on one side, and alphabet and numbers on the other, in original labeled Milton Bradley box. All good condition. Two puzzles complete. Mid-19th century. $500/700

248. Collection of Whistles and Little Toys

3" (8 cm.) h. doll top. Including three metal bird whistles, one horse head whistle, carved bone whistle, tin flute, tin white with lithographed

tin rattle, bisque doll with brown sculpted hair on metal "skirt" with finial base designed for use as spinning top, marked Poupée, Brevete SGDG, and a tin whistle with papier-mâché head having hinged mouth that opens when the whistle is blown. Very good condition. Late-19th century. $300/500

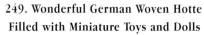

249. Wonderful German Woven Hotte Filled with Miniature Toys and Dolls

5 ½" (14 cm.) overall. The woven flat-back basket with rounded front ("hotte") is filled with wonderful early/mid-19th century dolls and toys including early papier-mâché lady with painted bonnet and wooden body, bisque head man with sculpted green Tyrolean hat and painted moustache, all-bisque Polichinelle with jointed limbs, and six early Erzebirge wooden toys including jointed cat, man on camel and boy on rocking horse. Excellent condition. Germany, mid/late-19th century; the hotte basket was the traditional method by which doll parts and supplies were delivered to home workers, and, when finished, returned to the main factory centers. The fascinating story of Ernestine Brandt, a famous hotte delivery woman during the late 1800s in Germany, is told in Cieslik's *German Doll Encyclopedia*. A rare and wonderfully-preserved miniature accessory. $700/900

250. German Wooden Doll Trunk with Dolls and Toys

8" (20 cm.) A wooden trunk with lithographed paper cover in Scottish plaid design, contains three small bisque dolls with glass eyes, painted features, open mouth, tiny teeth, brunette mohair wig, five-piece papier-mâché body, the larger marked Halbig K*R Germany 17, and each wearing its factory original Scottish costume. Along with various toys, viz., miniature teddy panda by Schuco, Hohner harmonica in original box, tiny bisque doll, papier-mâché ram with flannel cover and horns, tin penny toy train car, and two Erzebirge toys. Excellent condition. A delightful presentation of dolls and toys, with Scottish plaid theme, in Scottish decorated trunk. Germany, circa 1910. $600/900

251. German Pull-toy Cow on Wooden Platform

15" (38 cm.) The carved wooden cow has cream and tan hide cover, umber glass eyes, carved wooden horns, leather harness, and painted wooden hooves, and is mounted upon a wooden platform with cast iron wheels. Very good condition, very minor wear to hide at a few places. Germany, circa 1885. $700/900

253. Two German Porcelain Dolls with Furniture and Accessories

10" (25 cm.) dolls. Each doll has porcelain shoulder head with black sculpted hair, painted facial features, muslin body, porcelain lower limbs, painted shoes, antique costume. Condition: generally excellent. Comments: Germany, circa 1880, one doll has beautiful pink-tinted complexion and short ringlet curls, the other with sculpted ears, defined hair band and feathering around her forehead. Value Points: included is a three-piece set of diminutive doll furnishings in the cottage style with original finish, along with a porcelain wash bowl and accessories (original packing box of wash set included), and woven carpet. $700/1000

252. 19th Century American Midget Piano with Dancing Dolls

14" (36 cm.) h. The wooden piano with ebony finish and elephant-shaped cast iron legs has a display cabinet at the top with mirrored back that contains six miniature porcelain dolls. When the keys are played, a mechanism connects with the dolls which dance about. The piano is labeled "Gem" with gilt lettering, and has decoupage decorations. Very good condition, mechanism functions well, costumes a bit frail, finish on keys is worn. The enchanting American toy was patented in 1881 and is very rare to find. $1200/1600

254. Collection of French Miniature Accessories

2" (5 cm.) l. papeterie. Including early papeterie in folio style with gilt lettering, bone-handled fan with silk cover having decoupage or hand-painted scene, in original green paper case, bent wire basket with scene on base, two wooden hat stands with one early silk bonnet, folding fan with feather-trimmed blades, miniature book "Le Petit La Fontaine", another miniature book "Les Plaisirs de Campagne", leather folio, along with a German Walterhausen mirror with jewelry drawer. Good condition overall. French, perfect

for display with small bébés or classic poupée, mid/late-19th century. $400/600

255. Collection of German Soft Metal Doll Carriages

5" (13 cm.) Each of soft metal with elaborately detailed scroll designs, including carriages, two large strollers that might also be wheelchairs, and one tiny carriage with ivory finish. Each with original finish, two with bisque dolls. Very good condition. Germany, circa 1910. $500/700

256. Two Tiny German Porcelain Dolls with Wooden Articulated Bodies

3" (8 cm.) Each has porcelain shoulder head with black sculpted hair, painted facial features, shapely wooden torso and wooden upper arms and legs, porcelain lower arms and legs, dowel-jointing at shoulders, elbows, hips and knees. Condition: generally excellent. Comments: Germany, circa 1850. Value Points: the rare wooden-bodied dolls are notable for variation in hair styles, well-preserved condition, one with original costume, and each with early woven cradle. $700/1000

257. Four German Bisque Dollhouse Ladies with Ensemble of Dollhouse Furnishings

6" (15 cm.) Each doll has bisque shoulder head with painted facial features, mohair wig, muslin body, bisque lower limbs, painted shoes, and original factory costume of the Edwardian era. Condition: generally excellent. Comments: Germany, circa 1910. Value Points: the elegant party of women are arranged with a bountiful and beautifully-preserved set of German wooden dollhouse furnishing with fine natural finish and silver knobs, comprising glass-door cupboard, bookcase with attached etagere, hall mirror with marble shelf, wash stand with marble top and back, four drawer chest with attached mirror, and sewing table with velvet-lined drawer and two chairs. $1100/1500

258. Wonderful Set of French Maple Wood Bedroom Furnishings in Petite Size

12" (30 cm.) h. armoire. Each is of fine maple wood with natural finish and having faux-bamboo styled edging, comprising mirrored-door armoire, bed with canopy top, and four pieces with white marble tops, viz, four drawer tall chest, three-drawer chest, toilette table and night stand. Excellent condition. French, circa 1885, the set is especially desirable for its rare petite size. $700/1000

259. Pretty French Bisque Bébé by Jumeau, Size 1, with Dramatic Large Eyes

11" (28 cm.) Bisque socket head, large blue glass paperweight inset eyes, dark eyeliner, lushly-painted lashes, widely-arched brush-stroked brows, accented eye corners and nostrils, closed mouth with richly-shaded lips, pierced ears, auburn

mohair wig over cork pate, French composition and wooden eight-loose-ball-jointed body with straight wrists. Condition: generally excellent. Marks: Depose Tete Jumeau Bte SGDG 1 (and artist checkmarks, on head). Jumeau Medaille d'Or (body). Comments: Emile Jumeau, circa 1888. Value Points: the large eyes are enhanced by richly painted lashes and brows, lovely antique costume, undergarments, and velvet bonnet. $2800/3800

260. French Maple Wood Toilette Table with Porcelain Accessories

12" (30 cm.) Maple wood toilette table with natural finish, faux-marble top, two towel bars, bottom shelf, center drawer, has faux-bamboo carved edging. Resting atop the table is a set of white porcelain accessories with beautiful cobalt blue decorations of garlands, vines and birds. Excellent condition. French, circa 1890. $500/700

261. English Mahogany Pedestal Doll Table with Tableware

5" (13 cm.) Round mahogany table with pedestal base, and with ability to form into a tilt-top table, is laden with various table ware include porcelain dishes with blue and gilt borders (five plates, sauce dish with underplate, relish dish, and two oval bowls), along with four silver plate, and very fine silver cutlery (six knives and spoons, five forks), silver serving funnel, and a soft metal cruet set with two blown glass blue bottles. Excellent condition. Late-19th century. $400/600

262. German Bisque Miniature Doll with Lustre Boots in Original Costume, with Furnishings

3 ½" (9 cm.) Bisque shoulder head depicting young child with blonde sculpted hair,

painted features, muslin body, bisque lower limbs, painted stockings with purple tassels and purple lustre ankle boots, original blue silk dress and pantalets. Condition: generally excellent. Comments: Germany, circa 1870. Value Points: rare and beautifully-preserved miniature doll, including woven carpet, cream doll carriage with original sunshade, and two wooden chairs with blue silk upholstered seats. $300/500

263. French Bisque Bébé by Jules Steiner with Original Signed Body

12" (30 cm.) Bisque socket head, blue glass paperweight inset eyes, painted lashes, feathered brows, rose-blushed eye shadow, accented nostrils and eye corners, closed mouth with outlined lips, pierced ears, blonde mohair wig over Steiner pate, Steiner composition body with jointing at shoulders, elbows, and hips, pretty costume, bonnet, muff, undergarments, stockings, and shoes. Condition: generally excellent. Marks: A 5 Le Parisien Paris (head) (original Steiner body stamp). Comments: Jules Steiner, circa 1890. Value Points: charming bébé with eager expression, original pate, body, body finish, lovely bisque. $2500/2800

264. French Bisque Wide-eyed Bébé by Henri Delcroix with Little All-Bisque Doll

12" (30 cm.) Bisque socket head, very large blue glass paperweight inset eyes, lushly-painted lashes, wide brush-stroked and feathered brows, accented nostrils and eye corners, closed mouth with accented lips, pierced ears, brunette mohair wig over cork pate, French composition and wooden eight-loose-ball-jointed body with straight wrists, wearing antique flannel costume with embroidery, undergarments, bonnet, knit stocks and white kidskin boots. Condition: generally excellent. Marks: Paris 30 (head). Comments: Henri Delcroix, circa 1890. Value Points: rare to find doll with most expressive features, original body, choice bisque and painting, fine costume, and carrying her own little all-bisque doll. $2800/3800

265. Rare Petite German Brown-Complexioned Bisque Character, 1358, by Simon and Halbig

10" (25 cm.) Bisque socket head with sienna-brown complexion, brown glass sleep eyes, dark painted lashes, black feathered brows, accented nostrils and eye corners, open mouth, coral-shaded lips, four porcelain upper teeth, pierced ears, black mohair wig, brown composition and wooden ball-jointed body, wearing pretty antique costume, bonnet, undergarments, socks and shoes. Condition: generally excellent. Marks: 1358 1 ½. Comments: Simon and Halbig, circa 1910. Value Points: the model is rarely found, and is virtually unknown in this petite size, with very fine bisque and modeling, original body and body finish. $3000/4000

266. German All-Bisque Doll with Pink Lustre Slippers, and Tiny Set of Wooden Furnishings

3" (8 cm.) One-piece all-bisque doll depicting a young girl, with brown sculpted hair in short curls, painted features, chubby body, painted pink lustre boots and stocking tassels, antique lace dress with ribbon trim, and holding her own tiny doll. Condition: generally excellent. Comments: Germany, circa 1870. Value Points: rare doll model with enchanting expression, along with a set of German diminutive carved wooden furniture in the Gothic style, including hall mirror with cupboard base (mirror cracked), etagere with cupboard base and drawers, desk, pedestal table, sofa (one leg replaced) and three chairs with original brown leather upholstery, circa 1890. $300/600

267. German All-Bisque Mignonette with Canopy Bed

5" (13 cm.) Bisque swivel head on kid-edged bisque torso, cobalt blue glass eyes, closed mouth, painted features, peg-jointed bisque arms and legs, painted stockings and two-strap shoes, blonde mohair wig, antique chemise and pantalets.

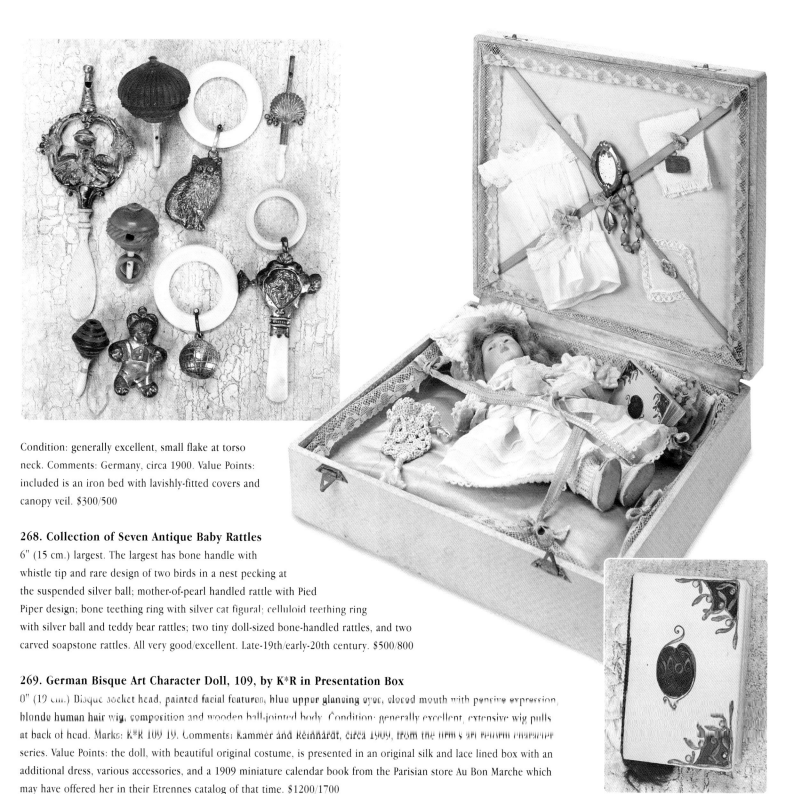

Condition: generally excellent, small flake at torso neck. Comments: Germany, circa 1900. Value Points: included is an iron bed with lavishly-fitted covers and canopy veil. $300/500

268. Collection of Seven Antique Baby Rattles

6" (15 cm.) largest. The largest has bone handle with whistle tip and rare design of two birds in a nest pecking at the suspended silver ball; mother-of-pearl handled rattle with Pied Piper design; bone teething ring with silver cat figural; celluloid teething ring with silver ball and teddy bear rattles; two tiny doll-sized bone-handled rattles, and two carved soapstone rattles. All very good/excellent. Late-19th/early-20th century. $500/800

269. German Bisque Art Character Doll, 109, by K*R in Presentation Box

0" (19 cm.) Bisque socket head, painted facial features, blue upper glancing eyes, closed mouth with pensive expression, blonde human hair wig, composition and wooden ball-jointed body. Condition: generally excellent, extensive wig pulls at back of head. Marks: K*R 109 19. Comments: Kammer and Reinhardt, circa 1909, from the firm's art reform character series. Value Points: the doll, with beautiful original costume, is presented in an original silk and lace lined box with an additional dress, various accessories, and a 1909 miniature calendar book from the Parisian store Au Bon Marche which may have offered her in their Etrennes catalog of that time. $1200/1700

113

270. Eight German All-Bisque Dolls with Original Costumes

3 ½" (9 cm.) Each is all bisque with one-piece head and torso, pin-jointed bisque arms and legs, painted stockings and shoes or boots, tiny glass eyes, painted features, closed mouth, mohair wig. Condition: generally excellent. Comments: Germany, circa 1900. Value Points: each child wears its factory original costume including fashionable child costume or folklore style. $1100/1500

271. Two German All-Bisque Characters with Teddy Bears

5" (13 cm.) Each has bisque swivel head on bisque torso, brown or blue glass sleep eyes, painted features, loop-jointed bisque arms and legs, painted shoes and socks, mohair bobbed wig; one with open mouth and two upper teeth, and the other with smiling expression on closed mouth, each well costumed. Condition: generally excellent. Comments: Germany, circa 1915. Value Points: each of the cheerful pair with expressive character features owns her own firm-bodied brown mohair teddy bear. $600/900

272. Four German Brown-Complexioned Bisque Dolls

7" (18 cm.) largest. Including bisque socket head girl, brown glass sleep eyes, painted facial features, open mouth, row of teeth, black mohair wig, brown composition and wooden fully-jointed body, nicely costumed, marked "34.16"; along with 5" all-bisque doll with brown glass eyes, solid neck, loop-jointed arms and legs, bare feet, black fleecy wig, marked "5/0"; and a pair of 3" all-bisque twin boy and girl each with painted hair and features, jointing at arms and legs, unusual orange painted shoes, and original factory costume, the girl with side-glancing eyes. Condition: generally excellent. Comments: Germany, early-20th century. Value Points: delightful group of a girl with her little dolls, seated on woven bench (included). $500/800

273. Small German All-Bisque Black-Stocking Girl with Filigree Metal Furniture

4" (10 cm.) Bisque swivel head on bisque torso, peg-jointed bisque arms and legs, black thigh-high painted black stockings, brown one-strap shoes, brown glass eyes, painted features, closed mouth, blonde mohair wig, pretty antique dress. Condition: generally excellent. Comments: attributed to Simon and Halbig, circa 1890. Value Points: especially pretty face, included are six pieces of filigree metal doll furnishings including high chair (to re-issue to child's rocker), carriage, table and two chairs, and fancy settee. $400/600

274. Petite Rare German Bisque Character Doll, 1478, by Simon and Halbig

10" (25 cm.) Bisque socket head, brown glass sleep eyes, painted lashes, one

stroke tapered brows, accented nostrils, closed mouth with very full outlined lips, pierced ears, blonde mohair wig, composition and wooden ball jointed body, wearing factory-original chemise dress, stockings, shoes and pretty antique bonnet. Condition: generally excellent. Marks: 1478 S&H 2. Comments: Simon and Halbig, circa 1910. Value Points: rare model with very beautiful expression and bisque, original body and body finish. $2800/3500

276. Set, German Papier-mâché Circus Animals in Original Box

11" (28 cm.) x 8" box. A firm-sided box whose lid has colorful engraving of circus animals and performer while a crowd looks on, contains original green leafy ground in which are arranged papier-mâché animals, including two alligators, elephant, bear, white polar bear, tiger, and lion, along with a black papier-mâché trainer with colorful costume. Excellent, unplayed with, condition. Germany, circa 1890. $300/600

277. Two German All-Bisque Dolls with Sculpted Top Hats

4" (10 cm.) Each is all-bisque with one-piece head and torso, sculpted black top hat above sculpted blonde hair, painted facial features, the larger with sculpted moustache, pin-jointed bisque arms and legs. painted black boots, antique costume. Condition: generally excellent. Comments: Germany, circa 1890. Value Points: rare modeled top hats. $300/500

275. Two Early Teddy Bears in Early Stenciled Wooden Cradle with Quilt

13" (33 cm.) larger bear. Two early mohair teddies with shoe-button eyes are resting in a 16" wooden cradle with original painted finish (red interior, dark blue exterior with gold pencil stripe), along with an early pieced quilt. Fair/good condition of teddies and quilt, cradle excellent. Early-20th century. $400/600

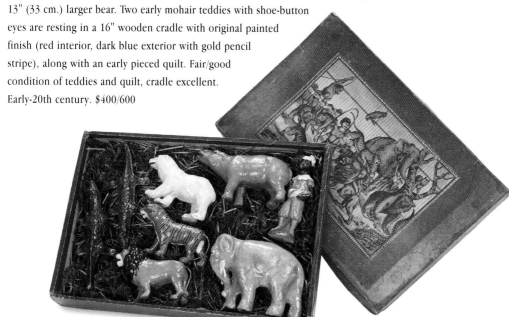

278. Early Mohair Teddy with Costume, Along with Collection of Teddy Bear Books

18" (46 cm.) Golden mohair teddy with unusual possum-shaped triangular face, embroidered flat nose, amber glass eyes, swivel head, jointed limbs with stockinette paw pads is wearing wire-rim spectacles, an old cotton romper suit and a brooch with chain and mother-of-pearl watch face. Condition: very good. Comments: early-20th

century. Value Points: very unusual facial modeling on the charming bear, along with a collection of early teddy bear books for children in fair/good condition including five volumes by Seymour Eaton, circa 1908 (*The Roosevelt Bears Abroad*, *The Traveling Bears in England*, *The Traveling Bears Across the Sea*, *More About Teddy B and Teddy G the Roosevelt Bears*, and *Teddy B* and *Teddy G the Bear Detectives*)., along with the complete 8 book series *The Teddy Bears* published by Reilly & Britton, Chicago, copyright 1907. $500/800

279. American Boxed Puzzle "St. Nicholas A.B.C. Picture Blocks" by McLoughlin Bros.
13" (33 cm.) x 7". A set of 24 wooden blocks have colorful lithographed scenes on two sides, one side with alphabet letter and a scene symbolizing that letter, (e. g. "D is for Dolly at a Dinner Party"), and the other side with scene as shown on the box lid cover. Excellent condition, complete, vibrant colors. McLoughlin Bros, New York, copyright 1887. $300/500

280. Eight German Bisque Dollhouse Men with Variations in Hair Style

5" (13 cm.) Each has bisque shoulder head with sculpted hair, painted facial features, muslin body, bisque lower limbs, antique or original costume. Condition: generally excellent, one broken foot. Comments: Germany, circa 1910. Value Points: wide variety of styles is shown, including Grandpa with bald pate, three men with black hair and moustaches with variations in each hair style, brown haired man with moustache, brown haired man with center-parted hair and long sideburns, brown-haired man with moustache and beard, and black-haired man with extended full sideburns that form into a moustache. $600/1200

281. German Bisque Miniature Gentleman with Sculpted Top Hat, with Fireplace

5" (13 cm.) Bisque shoulder plate depicting a gentleman, with sculpted black top hat, blonde hair, painted features, closed mouth, thin moustache, muslin body, bisque lower limbs, painted black boots, antique costume. Condition: generally excellent. Comments: Germany, circa 1885. Value Points: rare sculpted hat and moustache, included is an early mid-19th century pressed brass fireplace, mantel and fender, with arched crest and mirrors. $400/600

282. Collection of Miniature Steins

3" (8 cm.) tallest stein. Including seven lidded steins in various styles, the largest a figural cast metal stein signed L. Ostermayer Nurnberg and two glass steins with pewter lids and raised designs. Excellent condition. Germany, late-19th/early-20th century. $300/400

283. German Porcelain Doll with Glass Eyes

13" (33 cm.) Porcelain shoulder head with black sculpted hair having a wide center-part, then combed neatly behind her ears into short uniform finger curls, inset dark enamel eyes, red and black upper eyeliner, painted lashes, single stroke brows, closed mouth with pert smile, muslin stitch-jointed body, antique costume. Condition: generally excellent. Comments: Germany, circa 1860. Value Points: most charming expression lent realism by pink-tinted complexion, rare glass eyes. $400/600

284. A Well-Filled German Wooden Toy Grocery and Shop-Keepers

19" (48 cm.) l. x 11"h. A charming smaller-size wooden grocery has a back wall with eight spice drawers having porcelain German-language labels and paper borders to simulate inlay, a center shelved niche with mirrored back, fancy front columns with black stenciled trim, original lithographed paper floor, and original marbled counter. The shelves are laden with groceries, porcelain canisters, wooden ladder scales, cash register, along with many food stuffs, wooden telephone and wooden barrel on stand. There are three German bisque dollhouse people including shop-keeper with long grey beard, his grey-haired wife, and another woman, each with factory-original costumes. Excellent condition, original paper and painted finishes, some fading of wall papers. Germany, early-20th century. $2500/3500

285. German Dollhouse Telephones and Wireless Radios

2" (5 cm.) Including black gooseneck telephone, an unusual wooden wireless with headphones (one ear cap missing) and a card stock wireless with headphones. Very good/excellent condition. Germany, early-20th century. $200/300

286. German Dollhouse Clocks and 1887 Miniature Calendar

3" (8 cm.) tallest. Including pressed tin mantel clock with gold finish under original blown glass dome; cast metal mantel clock in burgundy and gold with figural statue (one urn design missing), and a gilt metal mantel clock with figural of young boy. Excellent condition but as noted. Germany, late-19th century. Along with a miniature wall calendar with tear-off months (January and February missing) for 1887 advertising E.N Denison & Co, Reliable Dealers in Diamonds, Watches and Jewelry". $300/500

287. Early German Dollhouse Dolls with Furniture and Accessories

5 ½" (14 cm.) lady. Including two bisque dolls each with shoulder head, sculpted blonde hair, painted features, muslin body, bisque lower limbs, the woman with painted black hair band and sculpted ears, wearing factory original costume. Condition: generally excellent. Comments: Germany, circa 1885. Value Points: fine all-original doll, included is marble top dollhouse table, chair, pair of silver metal candelabra, and lavender decanter with five glasses. $300/500

288. Two German Bisque Dollhouse Dolls and Furnishing

6" (15 cm.) man. Two bisque shoulder head dolls with sculpted hair, painted facial features, muslin body, and bisque lower limbs, including rare early woman with brown sculpted hair waved away from her face and held by a modeled snood, who is wearing her original costume; and a gentleman with sculpted full moustache, in formal wear suit. Condition: generally excellent. Comments: Germany, late-19th century, the woman circa 1870. Value Points: rare models, one in original costume, along with Waltherhausen wooden desk with ebony and gilt finish. $500/800

289. Small German Bisque Lady with Original Costume and Furnishings

5" (13 cm.) Bisque shoulder head of adult lady with pale blonde sculpted hair waved away from her face into short curls held by a black hair-band, painted features, tiny blue eyes, closed mouth, muslin body, bisque lower arms and legs. Condition: generally excellent, one foot and one hand broken. Comments: Germany, circa 1870. Value Points: especially fine detail of facial modeling and painting, very fine original gown with extended train. Included is a four-piece ensemble of wooden furnishings for the French market. $300/600

290. Very Rare French Bisque Bébé, Series G, by Jules Steiner

10" (25 cm.) Bisque socket head with elongated face, small blue glass enamel eyes, dark eyeliner, painted curly lashes, rose-blushed eye shadow, brush-stroked and fringed brows, accented nostrils and eye corners, closed mouth with outlined lips, pierced ears, blonde mohair wig, cork pate, Steiner composition fully-jointed body, lovely antique costume comprising dress, undergarments, stockings, leather shoes, and lace and frou-frou ribbon bonnet. Condition: small chip at corner and braid of chown area only into faint hairline to nose, one baby finger missing. Marks: Sie G 3/0. Comments: Jules Steiner, his Series G bébé, circa 1882. Value Points: very rare model by the firm with gorgeous face and painting, original body and body finish, lovely costume and presence. $2500/3500

292. Early Wax Moorish Miniature Man in Original Costume

8" (20 cm.) Solid wax head with wooden dowel attachment to torso has black bead eyes, well-defined handsome features, muslin body, wooden lower arms and legs with black complexion, painted orange boots. Condition: generally excellent, wig very sparse. Comments: early-19th century. Value Points: rare figure with especially fine detail of minute facial features, original well-preserved complexion, original homespun costume. $200/400

291. Two 19th Century Cloth Nannies with Babies

8" (20 cm.) larger. Each is of tightly-woven muslin with stitch-shaped nose and embroidered features, stitched-on thread hair, all-cloth hand-sewn body. Condition: generally excellent. Comments: mid-19th century, the dolls are shown and discussed in Ackerman's *Dolls in Miniature*, page 44. Value Points: each doll wears her original simple cotton dress and apron, and is holding a similarly made miniature cloth baby. $300/600

293. Very Rare German Wooden Peddler's Caravan by Gottschalk with Bountiful Wares

14" (40 cm.) The one-room wooden caravan with wooden wheels has a back porch with columns and railing, filled with wooden-potted flowers (with metal and wooden lawn mower). There are two windows at each side of the caravan with green painted shutters and original curtains. One side hinges open at mid-wall to form an upper front roof while the bottom half of the wall folds down to reveal a sample of the peddler wares. The one-room interior is fitted with a curved display shelf with paper lithograph cover in the same pattern as the wall papers, and the floor is covered with lithographed paper to simulate wood. The shelf, floor and walls are filled with a bounty of antique peddler wares. A bisque head dollhouse gent with original costume stands in attendance. Very good condition, one corner edge of roof has wood chip original finishes and papers overall, albeit some fading and rubs. Germany, Moritz Gottschalk, circa 1910, a very rare model by that firm with wonderful contents. $2500/3500

294. French Papier-mâché Poupée with Sturdy Body

15" (38 cm.) Papier-mâché shoulder head with black painted pate and feathered detail of hair around her face, black enamel eyes, painted features, open mouth, two rows of tiny teeth, shapely kid poupée body with gusset-jointing at hips and knees, stitched and separated fingers, wearing antique undergarments, apron, stockings, leather slippers. Condition: very good, two light craquelure lines on shoulder plate, original finish well-preserved, very sturdy body. Comments: French, circa 1850. Value Points: the early poupée, preceding the bisque and porcelain models, has finely made hand-stitched body and embroidered costume elements. $400/600

coffee service of turned wood with original cream and orange finish, including lidded coffee pot, creamer, vase, two cups and saucers. Good condition, some rubs on tin furniture. Germany, late-19th century, rare to find. $400/500

295. German Painted Tin Kitchen Furnishings and Erzebirge Wooden Dishes

4" (10 cm.) l. table. Each furnishing of tin with painted and stenciled finish to simulate wooden grain, including table, two chairs, hanging rack, barrel, wash tub, and a bench with stenciled message in old-style Germanic script. Along with a

296. Six German Dollhouse Fireplaces or Stoves

4" (10 cm.) Including two cast iron fireplaces (one with brass fender, and one with cast figural design; tin fireplace with soft metal gilded fender and lining, wooden fireplace with gilded soft metal trim, tinplate parlor stove with brass door and trim, and an unusual circular tin stove (may be incomplete). Very good condition. Germany, late-19th century. $800/1200

297. Collection of Early Doll Ephemera

4" (10 cm.) h. largest album. Included is an early leather covered writing set with hand-blown glass ink bottles, leather "Album" with 35 stamp-sized tintypes, porcelain ink well, another album with tintypes, tiny silk folio with stationery, pressed tin faux clock with easel back, seven leather bound volumes of Shakespeare, and wooden abacus. Fair/good condition. 19th century. $300/600

298. German Bisque "Old Lady Who Lived in A Shoe" with Little Dolls

5" (13 cm.) A hand-cobbled leather shoe with wooden sole is filled with a bisque doll as "the old lady" with blonde sculpted hair and black hair band, original body and costume, and all her eleven children, of bisque, porcelain and wood. Excellent condition. Mid-19th century. $300/500

299. German Papier-mâché Miniature Doll in Original Costume

6" (15 cm.) Papier-mâché shoulder head with painted short black hair having curls around the forehead, painted facial features, tiny blue eyes, closed mouth, muslin stitch jointed body. Condition: generally excellent. Comments: Germany, circa 1850. Value

Points: rare small size of this model with perfectly-preserved original finish, wearing original green flannel costume, boots, cap, leather strap. $300/500

300. Rare Small English Poured Wax Child in Early Wooden Cradle

6 ½" (17 cm.) Solid domed poured wax shoulder head with painted brown hair having feathered curls around her forehead, tiny blue glass bead eyes, painted features, muslin body, poured wax lower limbs, painted stockings and flat black ankle boots with red lacing, with original undergarment and skirt. Condition: generally excellent. Comments: English, circa 1850, the doll is shown in Ackerman's *Dolls in Miniature*, page 57. Value Points: rare size with beautifully-painted hair, original body with rare painted shoes. Included is an early wooden cradle with original painted decorations. $300/600

301. Three German Bisque Dollhouse Dolls with Rare Chairs

6" (15 cm.) Each of the dolls has a bisque shoulder plate, muslin body, bisque lower arms, painted shoes or boots, including lady with glass eyes and blonde mohair wig in rococo style (S&H 1160 model), woman with brunette mohair wig and painted features, full bisque arms, wearing original uniform; and man with sculpted hair, wearing original chauffeur's uniform. Condition: generally excellent, finger tip chipped on maid. Comments: Germany, circa 1900. Value Points: three rarely-found dollhouse models, along with a pair of handmade carved wooden chaise chairs with graceful shape. $500/700

302. Five Petite German Bisque Dollhouse Dolls with Furnishings

5" (13 cm.) Each has bisque shoulder head with sculpted hair, painted facial features, muslin body, bisque lower limbs with painted shoes. Condition: generally excellent. Comments: Germany, circa 1900. Value Points: the family group includes grey-haired older woman, bald older man, two young women with brown sculpted hair, and black-haired man with moustache, each wearing factory original costume. Included is seven-piece set of parlor furniture with padded upholstery and braided edging. $600/800

303. German Wooden Dollhouse Furnishings

7 ½" (19 cm.) h. dresser with mirror. Nine maple wood furnishings with natural finish are included, with silver knob hardware, including matched pair of beds with mattresses, marble top wash stand, marble top table, desk with slant top, settee with woven rush seat, dresser with hinged mirror, tea table, and armoire with mirrored door. Excellent condition. Germany, circa 1890. $500/800

304. Four German Bisque Dollhouse Dolls Depicting Elderly Persons

6" (15 cm.) Each has bisque shoulder head with sculpted hair and painted facial features, muslin body, bisque lower limbs, painted shoes. Condition: generally excellent. Comments:

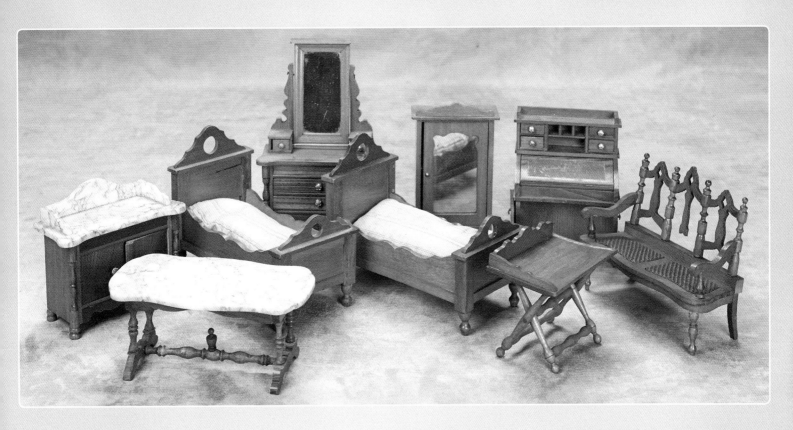

Germany, circa 1890. Value Points: included are two women with sculpted grey hair, a gentleman with bald pate and long grey sideburns, and a gentleman with grey beard, each with original costume. $400/700

305. Seven German Bisque Dollhouse Dolls on Presentation Board

4" (10 cm.) -5". Each has bisque shoulder head with sculpted hair, painted facial features, muslin body, bisque lower limbs, painted boots, undressed, and attached to wooden presentation board. Condition: generally excellent. Comments: Germany, circa 1900. Value Points: including various family members ranging from young man with side burns, brown-eyed man with moustache, elderly man with bald pate and sideburns, three various women, and young child. $500/700

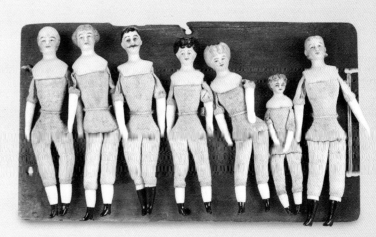

306. German Bisque Lady with Sculpted Hair, With Furnishings and Dishes

5 ½" (14 cm.) Bisque shoulder head with blonde sculpted hair in short casual curls, blue hair bow, painted facial features, muslin body, bisque lower limbs, unusual painted black ankle boots with green bows, antique costume. Condition: generally excellent, body repaired at waist. Comments: Germany, circa 1870. Value Points: rare to find this model in this small size; included is a wooden serving table with gold paper beading, along with Erzebirge wooden dishes having original ochre and blue painted finish. $300/600

307. Four Petite 19th Century German Bisque Dolls and Furnishings

4 ½" (11 cm.) largest. Each doll has bisque shoulder head with blonde or brown sculpted curls arranged in elaborate coiffure, painted facial features, muslin body, bisque lower limbs, painted shoes, and is wearing (frail) original costume. Condition: generally excellent. Comments: Germany, circa 1870. Value Points: miniature early sculpted hair dolls are rarely found, these including lady with three gold and black hair bands and painted earrings, lady with brown hair captured in seven horizontal rolls at the back of her head,

and lady with short brown finger-curled hair, along with little brown-haired boy with short curls. The woven carpet and two dollhouse furnishings are included. $400/600

308. Two German Bisque Dolls with Sculpted Hair and Blue Glass Eyes

10" (25 cm.) larger. Each has bisque shoulder head with very plump facial modeling, blonde sculpted short curly hair, cobalt blue glass eyes, painted features, closed mouth, muslin body, bisque lower legs, painted shoes, antique costume. Condition: generally excellent. Comments: Germany, circa 1880. Value Points: rare glass eyes particularly in the tiny model; the larger doll has excellent definition of hair, rare painted tan boots with black heels and turquoise tassels. $400/500

309. Two German Black-Complexioned Bisque Dolls

6" (15 cm.) and 7". Each has black bisque shoulder head with sculpted hair in short tight curls, painted facial features, the smaller with rarer painted brown

eyes, muslin body, bisque lower limbs, antique costume. Condition: generally excellent. Comments: Germany, circa 1900. Value Points: rare black-complexioned models with well-preserved complexions and painting, original bodies. $300/500

310. Collection of German Soft Metal Decorations

4" (10 cm.) h.
Christmas tree. Each is of soft metal, some with classic silvered finish, and others with vibrantly painted decorations, including dimensional figures, viz. Christmas tree, two pony carts with ponies, sleigh with double team of horses and drivers; and two-dimensional double-sided pieces, each with team of horse pulling a decorated parade cart, seven various plants or potted urns with colorful flowers, three soldiers a-horseback, and St. Nicholas. Excellent condition. $400/600

310.1. Two German Bisque Miniature Dolls and Donkey

4 ½" (11 cm.) Each doll has bisque shoulder head with sculpted hair, painted features, muslin body, bisque lower limbs. Condition: generally excellent. Comments: Germany, circa 1880. Value Points: each has original costume, including peddler lady with light brown hair, cotton costume, leggings, with market basket with two flannel fish; and little boy with dark brown hair and red flannel hooded suit with belt; along with flannel-covered donkey with harness and glass eyes. $300/500

311.

311. German Wooden Dollhouse Furnishings and Doll

7" (18 cm.) Maple-wood furnishings with fine natural finish and metal drawer pulls, includes pair of matched beds with mattresses, double door armoire, hall mirror, marble top chest, mirrored door cupboard, dressing table with marble top and mirror, and sofa with maroon velvet upholstery. Condition: generally excellent. Comments: Germany, circa 1890. Value Points: well-crafted furniture with marble top and original upholstery, included is bisque dollhouse lady with sculpted brown hair. $400/600

312. Two German Bisque Dollhouse Ladies with Tin Kitchen Furniture

5" (13 cm.) Each has bisque shoulder head with sculpted facial features and hair, muslin body, bisque lower limbs, painted shoes, and is wearing factory-original costume. Condition: generally excellent. Comments: Germany, circa 1900. Value Points: costumed as kitchen cooks or staff, also included is a stenciled and lithographed kitchen cupboard, table and two chairs $300/600

313. German Tin Toy Stove, Probably Bing

6" (15 cm.) (excluding pots). Designed to represent an early small gas stove, with

312.

313.

314.

315. Collection of Dollhouse Miniature Accessories

2 ½" (6 cm.) h. medicine chest. Including soft metal gilded Medicine Chest with raised lettering on door, the door hinging open to reveal five labeled glass medicine bottles; tin-framed table fan with wooden base; cast iron vacuum cleaner, and card stock wireless radio with glass bulbs and ear phones. Very good/excellent condition. Germany, circa1900. $400/700

316. German Miniature Specialty Lamp in Original Box

4" (10 cm.) A silver-finished metal lamp with modernist style has helmet-like shape, original cord, and blue bulb, and is presented in original box. Highly-stylized, the lamp evidently was designed with particular unidentified purpose. Mint condition in original box. Germany, early-20th century. $200/400

317. Two French Miniature Metal Street Lamps in Original Boxes

6" (15 cm.) A matched pair of cast metal street lamps have tin-lamp frames that enclose green or red glass shades; one glass panel hinges open for access to the interior. Good condition, some paint wear, one panel missing. The lamps are contained in their original boxes labeled "Made in France 5760". Early-20th century. $300/600

oven door, side door with tin sternum drawer, two original pots and lids that fit into burner holes at the stove top. Excellent condition. Germany, probably Bing, circa 1910. $300/500

314. Ten German Bisque Dollhouse Dolls Representing Various Family Members

6" (15 cm.) Each has bisque shoulder head with sculpted hair, painted facial features, muslin body, painted shoes and socks, wearing antique or original costume. Condition: generally excellent. Comments: Germany, circa 1910/20. Including are elderly people, one maid with mohair wig, one man with moustache, and several women with stylish bobbed hair of the 1920 era. $800/1300

315.

316.

317.

318. Two Petite German Bisque Dolls with Glass Eyes, with Lamb

5" (13 cm.) larger doll. Each doll has bisque shoulder head with blonde or brown sculpted hair, inset brown glass eyes, painted features, muslin body, bisque lower limbs with painted boots. Condition: generally excellent. Comments: Germany, circa 1885. Value Points: the rare small size of the early glass-eyed dolls that are wearing their factory-original costumes; included is papier-mâché lamb. $300/600

319. Two German Black-Complexioned Dolls and Papier-mâché Goat

6" (15 cm.) Including porcelain shoulder head doll with black complexion and sculpted black short curly hair, painted features, muslin body, black porcelain lower limbs, antique costume; all-bisque black child with swivel head and pin-jointed limbs, bare feet, painted facial features, black fleecy hair. Along with papier-mâché animal (goat?) with painted features. Excellent condition. Germany, late-19th century. $300/500

320. 19th Century American Children's Books and Games

10" (25 cm.) x 8" largest. Including *Kate Greenaway Almanack for 1884*; *McLaughlin's Wonderful Animal Book*; *Hire's Puzzle Book*; *Butterfly's Ball* by McLaughlin; boxed set of *Six Four Footed Friends* by Raphael Tuck; *The Metropolitan Mother Goose*; *Hansel and Grethel* published by B. Wilmsen of Philadelphia, printed in Germany; and *Babes of the Year* with illustrations by Maud Humphrey, published by Frederick Stokes. Good/very good condition. Late-19th century. $300/600

321. American Lithograph Cloth Goldilocks and the Three Bears by Kellogg

15" (38 cm.) x 16". Printed on crisp sateen muslin, the four sheets depict characters from the beloved fairy tale, each holding a bowl of cereal with "Kellogg's" name on the bowl, with instructions for making the doll, and with advertisement for the cereal company. Issued by Kellogg Co. of Battle Creek in 1926. Near mint condition, with crisp finish and vibrant colors. $200/400

322. American Carved Wooden Miniature Folk Doll

5 ½" (14 cm.) Carved wooden doll with highly-characterized features, painted black complexion, painted features, carved stuck-out tongue, wearing original handmade farmer's costume with wooden and tin hoe. Excellent condition. American, late-19th century. $200/300

323. Six Miniature Almanacs

2" (5 cm.) Including Hazeltine's Almanac for 1888,1889 and 1891; two copies of Piso's Almanac for 1906, and one for 1902. Good condition, very rare to find. $200/300

324. German Papier-mâché Cow with "Moo"

10" (25 cm.) The papier-mâché sculpted cow is mounted upon a wooden pull-toy platform with four cast iron wheels, and has bellows construction at the neck, which, when pushed, causes the cow to "moo", with amber glass eyes, horns, leather ears and tail, udder, leather collar. Very good condition brown flocked finish rubbed, one ear broken at tip, Germany, circa 1890. $400/600

325. Two German Bisque Miniature Dolls with Pull-Toy Animals

3 ½" (9 cm.) Including boy with bisque socket head, tiny glass eyes, closed mouth, painted features, wearing factory-original brown flannel suit with cap; along with girl with girl shoulder head and sculpted hair with black hair band, painted features, muslin body, factory original costume. Condition: generally excellent. Comments: Germany, circa 1890. Value Points: included are two papier-mâché pull-toys, camel and cow, on wheeled wooden bases. $300/500

326, 327.

326. Two French Wooden Doll Furnishings from Brittany

10" (25 cm.) Of very dark wood with elaborate floral and pinwheel carvings, the set comprises a bench with hinged seat for access to storage compartment, along with a cupboard with two sliding and two hinged doors, designed for use as bed compartment. Excellent condition. French, Brittany, early-20th century. $300/500

327. Two Petite French Bisque Bébés by Gaultier and Denamur

8" (20 cm.) Each has bisque socket head, blue glass paperweight inset eyes, painted features, closed mouth, accented lips, pierced ears, brunette mohair wig, French composition and wooden fully-jointed body, and each is wearing early chemise dress. Condition: each has faint forehead hairline. Marks: F. 2 G. (on one) E. 1 D. (the other). Comments: Gaultier Freres and Denamur, circa 1890. Value Points: charming size of the little bébés with original bodies and body finish. $800/1200

328. American Black Cloth Miniature Doll as Bride in Glass Dome

4" (10 cm.) Of black cotton sateen with rounded head, embroidered facial features, black thread hair, shapely torso and slender limbs. Condition: generally excellent. Comments: American late-19th/early-20th century. Value Points: wonderfully-preserved, the doll wears an original wedding gown and veil of gauzy scrim fabric, with paper floral bouquet, and is preserved under a blown glass dome. The doll is show and described in Ackerman's *Dolls in Miniature*, page 43. $300/500

329. Rare Miniature Game, Probably French

2 ¾" (7 cm.) x 1 ¾". A wooden box with marbled paper cover has a glass window front that protects an early hand-colored engraving depicting a woman seated at an easel, with brush in hand. The "painting" on the easel is actually a cut-out

328.

panel that exposes various views behind it in a rotating manner. Included with the simple game are four wooden panels with complete colored engravings of the drawings that are hinted at in the cut-out panel, including portrait of Victor Hugo, woman on bicycle, Eiffel Towel, and soldiers. Good condition. Probably French, circa 1890. $300/500

330. Petite French Bisque Bébé by Jumeau with Original Chemise, and With Armoire

11" (28 cm.) Bisque socket head, brown glass paperweight inset eyes, painted lashes, brush-stroked and feathered brows, accented nostrils and eye corners, closed mouth with outlined lips, pierced ears, (new) brunette human hair wig over cork pate, French composition and wooden fully-jointed body. Condition: generally excellent. Marks: 2

330.

(socket head) Jumeau Medaille d'Or Paris (body). Comments. Little Jumeau, circa 1890. Value Points: petite pretty brown eyed bébé with original signed body in impeccable condition, original muslin chemise, brown leather shoes, cap; included is a French wooden armoire with mirrored front door. $1700/2200

329.

331. Collection of Accessories for Bébé or Larger Poupée

11" (28 cm.) parasol. Including wooden-handled parasol with dog-head figural grip and original rose silk (frail) cover; another wooden-handled parasol, porcelain pitcher and pot with unusual berry and floral design, celluloid hanging mirror with accessories including unusual miniature celluloid whisk broom, green leather gloves, leather purse with bail handle, two mesh purses, wooden-framed hand mirror, wooden comb, woven double-sided basket, and celluloid comb. Excellent condition. Late 19/early-20th century. $400/600

332. Small German Wax Child Doll and Chairs

6 ½" (17 cm.) Wax over papier-mâché shoulder head with blue glass inset eyes, painted features, closed mouth, blonde mohair wig, muslin body, papier-mâché limbs with painted grey boots and red rimmed stockings, nicely costumed. Condition: very good, some fading of features. Comments: Germany, circa 1880. Value Points: rare small size of this model, original body with unusually-painted boots; along with set of four bentwood chairs with red velvet upholstery (one back leg missing) and velvet-covered miniature cat with original label "Made in Germany". $200/400

333. Good Collection of Eleven Early Miniature Purses

3" (8 cm.) l. blue purse. A fine variety with various designs and materials, including woven royal blue purse with gold accents and clasp; stiff wire mesh purse, black beaded purse with gilt beading, three crocheted purses (rose, brown and red) with gold closures, two silver purses, silver mesh purse, miser's purse, and embossed gold purse with red silk lining. Very good/excellent. 19th century. $400/700

334. Ensemble German Wooden Dollhouse Furnishings with Doll and Accessories

5 ½" (14 cm.) doll. 5"h. piano. All-bisque doll with one-piece bisque head and torso, brown glass sleep eyes, painted features, closed mouth, loop-jointed bisque arms and legs, painted shoes and socks, original blonde mohair wig, pretty silk dress, marked 150 3/0. Condition: generally excellent. Comments: Germany, circa 1900. Value Points: included is a 14-piece ensemble of parlor and dining room furniture with pressed designs and red mahogany finish, featuring chaise lounge and two chairs with original green flannel upholstery and braid trim, mirrored armoire, upright piano, dining table with hidden extension leaves, hanging clock, hall mirror, sewing table with velvet-lined drawer, and more. Along with a large assortment of German miniature blown glassware. $700/1000

335. Collection, 19th Century Miniature Desk Accessories

3 ¼" (8 cm.) clock. Including miniature framed engraving, cast metal gilded clock with Art Nouveau lady base, silver (hallmark) calendar frame with celluloid sheets of days and weeks, silver funnel, red enamel Austrian miniature purse with hand-painted scene, soft metal silvered double inkwell, tiny silver ring with three turquoise stones, knife, marbled green metal inkwell and blotter, bone implement, silver wallet with tiny sepia scenes of French history, and tiny1" book "Bijou Pictures of Paris" with early tiny engravings of historic sites. Late-19th/early-20th century. $400/600

336. German Bisque Miniature Doll with Swivel Head, and Toilette Table

5 ½" (14 cm.) Solid domed bisque swivel head on bisque shoulder plate, painted facial features, muslin body, long blonde mohair wig, bisque lower limbs and painted blue boots and ribbed stockings, undergarments. Condition: generally excellent. Comments: Germany, circa 1875. Value Points: the petite doll has rare swivel head variation and fancy boots, included is a Walterhausen wooden toilette table with gilt-accented ebony finish and attached mirror. $300/500

337. Two German Bisque Dollhouse Dolls

5" (13 cm.) Each has bisque shoulder head, muslin body and bisque lower limbs with painted shoes, including lady with blonde mohair wig and brown glass eyes who is wearing original silk gown, known as "Little Women" doll by Simon and Halbig; and man with black sculpted hair and moustache, and brown painted eyes in formal tuxedo. Condition: generally excellent. Comments: Germany, circa 1890. Value Points: the handsome couple are in hard to find petite size, with original costumes. $300/400

338. Eight German Bisque Dollhouse Dolls

5" (13 cm.) Each has bisque shoulder head with sculpted hair, painted facial features, muslin body, bisque lower limbs, and each is wearing factory-original costumes. Condition: generally excellent, slight surface dust to costumes. Comments: Germany, circa 1900. Value Points:

included are three elderly bald-headed men with variations in side burns, man as grocery clerk, man with sculpted grey fedora (tiny flake on brim), grey-haired woman with unusual pink stockings, and two women as house servants. $600/900

339. Five German Bisque Dollhouse Dolls in Original Costumes

6" (15 cm.) -7". Each has bisque shoulder head with painted facial features, muslin body, bisque lower limbs, painted shoes, and is wearing factory-original costume; with sculpted hair including man with moustache, and with mohair wig. Condition: generally excellent. Comments: Germany, circa 1900. Value Points: good family group with variety of persons, original costumes. $500/800

340. Tiny German All-Bisque Dolls and Metal Furnishings

2" (5 cm.) -3". Each of the five dolls is all-bisque with one-piece head and torso, pin-jointed limbs, painted hair and facial features, painted stockings, antique costume. Condition: generally excellent. Comments: Germany, circa 1920. Value Points including two little girls with sculpted bunny-ear hats, and two maids with sculpted white ruffled caps. Also included is a set of tiny metal furnishings in original green and gilt paint. $200/400

340.

341.

339.

341. Group German Dollhouse Accessories

2 ¼" (6 cm.) h. radiators. Including two silver soft metal chandeliers, embossed Germany, one with blue glass teardrop dangles; two cast metal radiators with original gilt finish; silver metal coffee samovar; cast metal five-arm candelabra; tin silvered hanging clock with swinging pendulum; gilt mantel clock with pendulum; gilt candelabra, and set of silver metal dishes with original paper label Therhgroom Excellent condition. Germany, early to mid-20th century $300/500

342. Collection of American Wooden Dollhouse Furnishings by Tynietoy

8" (20 cm.) corner cupboard. Including corner cupboard, high four poster bed, grandfather clock, folding screen with Japanese scene, nine-piece turquoise baby furniture with stenciling (one piece signed), wing chair, and pair of candlesticks each bearing Tynietoy signature but as noted. And two red ladder back chairs, black ladderback chair, wall clock, mantel clock and tilt-top chair table which are not signed but are attributed to Tynietoy. Excellent condition. American, Tynietoy, circa 1930. $300/600

343. Wooden Doll Table with Porcelain Dinnerware, and Other Dishes

10" (25 cm.) l. table. A country-style drop leaf pine table has porcelain tea service with orange and gilt accents, including lidded teapot, lidded sugar, creamer, six cups and saucers. Along with another fine porcelain (partial) service with unusual pattern of embossed holly berries and leaves, including lidded teapot, lidded sugar, two larger cups, small footed cup, three saucers or plates, two serving plates, creamer, and basket. Excellent condition. Germany, late-19th century. $200/400

344. Three German Porcelain Dollhouse Dolls

7" (18 cm.) Each has porcelain shoulder head with black sculpted hair, painted features, muslin body, porcelain lower limbs, and each is wearing pretty antique costume. Condition: generally excellent. Comments: Germany, circa 1875. Value Points: interesting variation of hair styles. $300/500

hot water bottle on original card, and another card with four miniature baby accessories including tin bed warmer. Good/very good condition. Early-20th century. $200/300

348. Five Early Glass Baby Bottles

7" (18 cm.) The clear glass baby bottles are each decorated with a raised design, one with a seated baby and the words "Happy Baby", and the others with embossed animals (cat, two dogs, and bunny). Excellent condition. Circa 1920. $100/200

349. Wonderful Collection of Early Celluloid Toys and Novelties

7" (18 cm.) l. horn rattle. Including two musical horns with

345. Two German All-Bisque Dolls and Playskool Pullman Coach Car

10" (25 cm.) h. The metal-sheet box-shaped coach car with original brown paint has two windows, painted panel with train car number A756 , and gold lettering "Playskool Pullman Sleep - Dolly - Sleep" on one side; the entire side hinges open to reveal the car interior with padded seats, table, bed, and closet with extra blankets. Circa 1920s. Included are two all-bisque dolls with glass eyes, closed mouth, mohair wig, pin-jointed arms and legs, painted yellow boots, one with swivel head, Germany, circa 1910. Excellent condition. $800/1000

346. Tiny German All-Bisque Babies in Layettes

2 ½" (6 cm.) l. dolls. Three pink-tinted all-bisque babies with pin-jointed bisque arms and legs, painted baby hair and facial features, original costumes, are presented in original woven basket layettes with original blankets. Dolls by Hertwig, circa 1920s. One of the baskets has original paper label "Park Avenue Doll Outfitters, Phila, Pa". Excellent condition, slight dustiness. $300/400

347. Collection, Vintage Baby Accessories

3" (8 cm.) bottle. Including one clear bottle with bone cap, La Petite Alpha Nursing Bottle in original box (along with an advertising for a nickel-plated liquid pistol, described as "not a toy"), rubber

attached figures of children on sled on one and a boy on rocking horse on the other, costumed duck, lamb with rare jointed legs, Santa and reindeer, dog, 'wicker' carriage, lamb on pull-toy base, five various roly-dollies including amusing poodle standing on his head and several clowns, four dolls with rattle handles or teething rings, Buster Brown and Dog, and fifteen various animals. Germany and Japan, 1910/1930s. $400/600

350. French Mechanical Drumming Bunny by Roullet et Decamps

13" (33 cm.) excluding ears. The papier-mâché standing bunny is lavishly covered with white fur, has amber glass eyes, tall bunny ears, and hinged arms. In right hand he holds a baton, and a drum is attached to his torso with cymbals. When wound, he beats the drum and claps the cymbals. The key has the R.D. initials of Roullet et Decamps. Excellent condition. French, circa 1915. $800/1200

351. Large Group of German Miniature Garden Furnishings by Karl Schreiter

7" (18 cm.) l. larger sofa. Including three different sets of miniature garden furnishings, with embossed designs to simulate woven wicker, each with sofa, two arm chairs and a round table, with various color trim. Along with four boxes of potted shaved-wood flowers in original boxes. Very good/excellent condition. Germany, Karl Schreiter, circa 1930s, a catalog of the furnishings is shown in the *Lexikion der Puppenstuben und Puppenhauser* by Cieslik and Kohler. $600/900

352. German Dollhouse Garden Furnishings

6" (15 cm.) The pressed card stock set with embossed designs to simulate woven wicker has original lime green painted finish with dark green trim, and includes tall cupboard with rounded front, two unusually-shaped ferneries (one with double layer of shelving), round table, sofa, hamper bench, and one chair. Very good condition. One piece is impressed Germany on underside. Circa 1920. $300/500

353. Collection of Early-20th Century German Toys and Novelties

5" (13 cm.) doll in chair. Including a bisque-head doll with sculpted hair and painted facial features, wooden block torso, tin arms, seated in a painted tin wheeled chair which, when moved along, causes the doll to clap its hands; cardboard candy container egg with images of Golliwog and penny wooden doll, woven double-lidded basket with three bisque half dolls by Hertwig having character like faces; ball of woven threads, wooden ball and stick toy, wooden

spinning top, woven rattle. Good to excellent, finish on the arms of doll in chair is very worn. Germany, early-20th century. $400/600

354. Thirteen German All-Bisque Flapper Era Dolls

3" (8 cm.) Pink-tinted all-bisque dolls with one-piece head and torso, sculpted blonde or brunette

hair, painted facial features, pin-jointed bisque arms and legs, painted orange socks and bright orange shoes. Condition: generally excellent. Comments: Germany, circa 1920. Value Points: the little flapper era dolls are wearing their factory-original costumes, each different. $400/600

355. German Bisque Pouting Character, 6969, by Gebruder Heubach with Puppy Doll

8" (20 cm.) Bisque socket head, painted facial features, dark blue intaglio eyes, red and black upper eyeliner, one stroke brows, closed mouth with downcast pouting lips, brunette mohair wig with side-coiled braids, five-piece papier-mâché body, painted shoes and socks, wearing antique costume. Condition: generally excellent. Marks: 6969 5/0 Germany, (somewhat) Gebruder Heubach, circa 1912, included with the little girl is a bisque-head puppy with painted side-glancing eyes, cloth body, antique dress. $800/1100

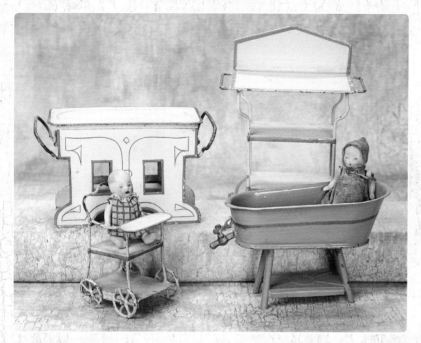

356. German Tin Baby Furnishings Attributed to Maerklin, with Babies

5" (13 cm.) Three tin bathroom furnishings with original cream paint and blue and gold accents, including changing cabinet with towel bars, tall shelving cabinet with towel bars, and wheeled baby chair with food tray. Along with a blue tin bathtub with gold stencil and drain faucet. Very good condition, some small flakes to the original painted finish. Germany, Maerklin, circa 1910. Included are two German all-bisque babies.
$500/800

357. German Bathroom in Original Cardboard Room with Wooden Furnishings, Along with Dolls

12" (30 cm.) l. box. A heavy stock box with decorative paper covers inside and out, hinges open at top and front to reveal a fitted bathroom, with wooden bathtub, sink, and toilet with attached paper roll. Included are three all-bisque babies with blonde painted hair and facial features. Excellent condition. Germany, circa 1920.
$400/600

358. Four Character Dollhouse Dolls in Original Costumes

6" (15 cm.) man. Each has sculpted head with highly-characterized painted facial features, mohair wig, cloth body, original costumes depicting three servants in upper-class 1900-era home, plush a little girl in night shift. Excellent condition. Maker and age uncertain. $300/500

359. Collection of American Tobacco Miniature Rugs

4" (10 cm.) x 2 ½". Collection of 23 miniature velvet carpets designed to appear as woven rugs, with silk fringe, some with original stamp on back "The Original Rug, Luxury Cigarettes..." Along with two larger examples. The carpets were given as premiums or promotional items with the purchase of cigarettes. Near mint condition. American, early-20th century. $200/400

360. American Metal Miniature Bathroom Set by Tootsietoy in Original Box

3 ½" (9 cm.) The vibrant cardboard box with colorful images of children playing with dollhouse furnishings contains within, in unplayed with condition, a set of metal bathroom furnishing with original lavender and cream painted finish, including bathtub, lidded toilet, lidded hamper, two chairs, sink, medicine chest, stool and scale. Excellent condition. Tootsietoy, the box is labeled "#50 Orchid Bathroom". Circa 1920s. $200/300

361. Set of Tin Lithographed Miniature Flossie Fisher Furniture as Candy Containers

3" (8 cm.) h. chairs. Five-piece matched set of dollhouse-sized furnishings are of tin with yellow lithographed finish having black silhouette designs inspired by the early child's book illustrations. Each piece is designed with access to the hollow interior which served as a candy container. Included is pedestal table, rocking chair, sidehoard and two straight chairs. Very good/excellent. Each piece is labeled Flossie Fisher's Funnies and the back of chairs are stamped "Geo Borgfeldt & Co, New York N.Y. Serial Number 2862 Net Wt ¼ oz". The Flossie Fisher Funnies, drawn by American artist Helen Nyce appeared in the Ladies Home Journal, circa 1911. $400/600

Immediately following lot #361 will be the auction of 100+ additional lots (samples shown above) from the Evelyn Ackerman Collection. Bidding on these additional lots will be available for attending bidders only.